PAINFUL
DEATH

THE LOSS OF A CHILD IS A PARENT'S WORST NIGHTMARE

DON'T LET THIS HAPPEN TO YOU!

PRINCE KAFAIN EMMANUEL MBENG, SR.

FOUNDER/PRESIDENT /CEO
MANNY'S EXECUTIVE SEDANS AND KEMCO INTL, INC.

PAGE PUBLISHING, INC.
Conneaut Lake, PA

First originally published by Page Publishing 2020

ISBN 978-1-66240-631-7 (pbk)
ISBN 978-1-66240-632-4 (digital)

Printed in the United States of America

I would like to dedicate this book to my son, Taku Mbeng, and my wife, Delphine, who both rushed in to help me with resuscitation when I found my boy unconscious. We all then realized that Junior must have given up the ghost with the three of us present at home, but practically unaware to be able to be of any remedial help. These two have since had to live with the memories of that fateful day, the trauma of which I wouldn't be doing them any justice if I fail to commend them for their bravery and poised involvement in our struggle for rapid intervention. They faced a very challenging and difficult experience on that particular evening, thus becoming my heroes; and for that, I am exceptionally grateful as I continue to ponder why it had not been my life that was taken away like that on that dreadful day. I also dedicate this book to my late sisters—Victorine, Joy, Angeline, and Irene— hoping that they would have received and checked our child in to the Kingdom of Heaven, as hopefully would be expected of any family member that God "calls" home first. His late uncle, Paul Mbeng, will definitely be happy "to finally fly" around the heavens with him, as I suppose or believe they do up there in the kingdom of heaven. Last, but not the least, I dedicate this book to Grace, Junior's mother, for the courage she has exuded so far in dealing with the nightmare of the loss of her child. Such loss is still the most difficult and devastating thing that any parent should have to face, and I wish her and all in our extended families peace, love, and happiness as they all seek ways to move on with their lives without the physical presence of Junior in it.

Taku Mbeng, first brave assistant responder, and Delphine Mbeng, second brave assistant responder

He didn't even get to tell me goodbye.

—Taku

So terrible, and so fast, but no time to intervene...thus leaving us with everlasting pain!

The loss of a child is truly the worst thing to happen to any parent.

—Daddy

CONTENTS

Lost still, in the maze in which we attempt an explanation of the unexplainable, Prince Kafain takes us on a journey through pathos, where, right before our very eyes, Junior takes an exit!! It is one of those perennial issues we forever grapple with, oscillating between the seesaw swings of haplessness and hopefulness. Steadily, and artfully in this book, Prince gets us on the latter. Reassured, we rise, dust ourselves, and look ahead.

MARTHA NGWAINMBI (PhD)

AUTHOR'S NOTE

It is with much disdain that I have chosen to express my anger and frustration about a painful loss—a loss that has altered the lives of all in the Mbeng/Chiabi/Abong families. Our son was quite healthy on that morning of June 29, 2018, but by the tail end of that day, all in my family would explode into mourning, because the same healthy loved child had gone to meet his maker. It is not my intention to question why the Lord chose to call him home on that particular day, for no answer will satisfy me now, nor bring him back to me. What I will try to do will be to tell his story in public, with the hope that his example will be helpful in preparing other families for such contingencies, should something similar come their way.

Our son Junior was unconditionally very special to Grace, Regina, and me, and to many others in our families; and very special because he commanded, attracted, and invoked varying qualities of child formation that always brought us together as family when all else went wrong. Junior wanted all of us to remain a united family, even against the odds of crucial circumstantial differences and difficulties; and to quote Rodney King in the Los Angeles riots in the nineties, who said, "Let's all get along," he, Junior, would tell me how important it was for everyone in our extended family to "just get along." He was an ambitious kid, and probably lacked the experience to read deep into adult shenanigans, but his focus on peace was equally and essentially vital, and in his mind, any absence of it could have caused him to extraordinarily deviate from the sanctimonious decency that was fundamentally prevalent in the trajectory of our family life. In his own volition, he made unwise and regrettable choices, and in our camaraderie of understanding, we all in the Mbeng and Abong families will never know why, or even if there was anything we missed, that could have averted the untimely departure of our lovely son.

As his father, and the inevitable authority that must keep his memories alive and dignified, I wish to absorb vicarious responsibility for every misstep in his life. I can confidently declare our unity in this devastating loss, as we tell the world that it was the will of God that he was given to us in 1993, and it is the will of God that he has been taken away from us in 2018. Junior will continue to abide in us, and his brother will continue to visit his grave when I am gone, and his memories will live on. In his honor, and his little but very important legacy, we are pleading that everyone should try to live in peace and pay great attention to the little indifferences that rip families apart, for there is always a way out, if and when we take the time to rethink and implore diligent compromises to pertinent family discrepancies and indiscretions. I now wish I had focused a little bit more on this factor or fact of life for my dear son's sake, but time is no longer of the essence for me now, but can be for you.

THE LOSS OF A CHILD IS A PARENT'S WORST NIGHTMARE!

Junior, Daddy, and Taku

He was brave; he was loved; he was bold; and he was caring. Some called him Bobe, some called him Emmanuel, and everyone knew him as Junior. He loved his mother a lot, his sister and nephew too, and his brother was his best friend. He always found ways to try to please his father, and his father gave him all the power to be responsible, wanting him to be in charge when he, his father, was absent. But somewhere, somehow, something went wrong, or maybe right, and God called him and then left me and my clan to wonder and wander around his glories that would have been. If only we had known how to read the signs and be able to call it off when we could, but it's too late now, and we just have to accept and be happy for his new life, that includes God and all loved ones who went before him. Fare-ye well, my boy!

HIS FINAL RESTING PLACE

He now rests in peace, and only he can differentiate the values and comforts of life on earth and in heaven. On behalf of his mother, his brother, his sister, his nephew, and everyone who cared about him, I, his father, wish to pray for his smooth transition into the kingdom of heaven, and plead that he should continue to shine down on us, and hope that he will represent us up here until we join him.

FOREWORD

The story of creation is a phenomenon that has two major opposing opinions. There is the religious position on creation described in the book of Genesis in the Bible, and on the opposite side is the scientific view that traces life to the big bang theory, followed by subsequent evolution. Whether one believes in the biblical or the scientific origins of life, and whether evolution is still ongoing or not, there is a mystery that always seems to force all human beings to question the origins and the purpose of human life. This mystery is death. Permit me, however, to state that to the best of my knowledge, life has two extremes or major mysteries, with the first one being birth, and the last one being death.

The author, Prince Kafain Emmanuel Mbeng, Sr. in this touching book has taken the readers through a journey that began with a lot of joy when, on September 7, 1993, he became a first-time dad. Becoming a first-time dad was a major achievement for Prince, and even more special because he had just become a dad to a boy who he believed would grow up and bury him, as is enshrined in the Kom culture where he hails from. He was overwhelmed with love and happiness and decided to share his name with his son, naming him Emmanuel Kafain Mbeng Jr. As news about Junior's birth spiraled, there was celebration from the USA to the Southern Cameroons, and to wherever Kafain and Grace had family and friends. Birth, though a mystery even in this age of family planning, never attracts any questions when compared to the mystery of death. This is probably so because it is human nature to celebrate not just new life, but anything new that adds to the family—be it a new car, a new home, a diploma, marriage, and many others.

Prince Kafain in this book demonstrates uncommon courage and applies lots of emotion in narrating a very intimate detail of what can only be described in summary by borrowing the title of the popular movie *The Good, the Bad and the Ugly*. In using this analogy, Junior's birth and childhood years prior to him becoming a teenager were not just "good" but excellent, as I personally knew and interacted with him during this period. Junior and his sibling, Taku, were two kids who were very adorable, well-behaved, and it was always fun to hang out with them. After the "good," Prince Kafain describes in this book a time that seems to represent the "bad," and this was the time when the father and son—or permit me to say parent-and-child relationship—experienced turbulence. Despite the turbulent times, Prince hoped that there would be a turnaround moment, but unfortunately, the "ugly" hit, and Junior was no more.

Following the author's perception, it is crystal-clear that nothing can be more devastating in life than losing a loved one, and particularly one's own child. No level of schooling or counseling can prepare anyone to be able to accept such a loss, and that is why no matter how many times that we have buried loved ones in the past, we can never get used to death, to be able to accept it without mourning. While the "good" memories of Junior's life serves as a pointer to the fact that every human being has a good seed in their heart, the memories of the "bad" and the "ugly," though painful, present many life lessons that could be useful for young people and parents who may find themselves in similar situations.

Dr. Ngeh J. Toyang
Chief Executive Officer
Flavocure Biotech Inc.
Baltimore, Maryland, USA

CHAPTER ONE

MY RANTS ON JUNIOR'S UNTIMELY DEPARTURE!

The death of a child has to be the worst experience in the life of a parent.

June 29, 2018, has become a remarkable day for Taku, Grace, Del, Li, and me—not forgetting Gil, Roy, Vic, Ka, and all family and friends of the Aaron and Johnson families. It has become a day in our lives reckoned not for the absence of the pleasures of life, but for sudden tragedy that untimely snatched precious life away from us, in a painfully dramatic way—a way that has made us famous, mainly for our resilience and will to continue living.

"He is sleeping," my younger son thought when I asked him to call his brother down for dinner; and in his innocence, he could never have thought that Junior was never going to wake up again. Taku and I went ahead and ate, and he then went back to his room, as they always do. Just a few minutes later, I instinctively decided to walk up to Junior's room—only to then find him unresponsive and unconscious. Difficult to know when he could have actually passed out. An attempt to wake him left me futile with screams that would invite Taku and Del to rush in and start assisting me with CPR, as was directed by the 911 attendant. In less than five minutes or so, the Fairfax County emergency team arrived, carried my boy in their ambulance, and Taku and I drove behind them, to the Mount Vernon General Hospital, where Junior would be pronounced dead.

Del had stayed back to assist some detectives with investigations and definitely still had hopes. And of course all this was happening so unbelievably fast to comprehend! We had parked the car at the hospital parking lot, and as we (Taku and I) walked into the ER, a nurse walked up to us, asked if I was Mr. Mbeng, and then walked us to a waiting room where a physician was going to come and talk to us. It immediately became evidently clear to me that the news was bad, and that Taku and I were never going to see our brother and son, respectively, alive again. The shock was catastrophic, and my heart immediately started boiling inside me.

Emotions instantly went into high gear, and I literally had to hold Taku down from breaking apart. He had lost recognition of me in his confused state of mind, so I reminded him who I was and who his brother was to me too, and immediately had to focus on his well-being, without showing him that I too was completely torn apart. Being Taku's best friend had to have made Junior very special to him, and the thought that his only brother was forever gone was going to create a big vacuum in his life, which even his father's love couldn't fill. I held my boy close to me and reminded him in a silent prayer that it was the will of God, and we were all going to be okay; and I could feel his heartbeat and fury calm down substantially. And of course we were still awaiting his mother's arrival—needless to say that her reaction to what had just happened would be explosive and painful to watch. What a traumatic experience for my little boy, whose brother had just died in our hands. What a traumatic experience for Del, whose new best friend's ghost had just departed in her hands. I was completely flabbergasted, wandering and wondering if I would be able to hold everyone together. There was absolutely no way I could have imagined that I would become a statistic of such trepidation, and there I was, wishing someone would tell me that I was just having a terrible dream.

Extreme anger had penetrated into my heart in very disgusting fashion, and though I managed to initiate a few calls, how I was going to deal with the crowd of relatives and friends that were now pouring in propped into my mind, especially noticing the general disbelief that was visible on every face. Silence was prevalent, and people spoke

14

in whispers, but Grace and Georgette couldn't hold back their display of emotions, understandably so—of course, they had just lost a child. Georgette had been upstairs taking care of patients in the same hospital, unaware that her nephew had just been pronounced dead there at the emergency room below, until Dominic, her husband, came and called her to rush down to the scene. The more I struggled to reflect on what to do, the angrier I became, and given the choice then, I would have chosen to go in Junior's place. Parents should not bury their children. Two weeks prior to that day, I had just briefed JR and Taku when they took me out to a fabulous Father's Day brunch in Fairfax that they needed to be strong and focused on their independence. I was a cancer survivor, and something could suddenly happen to me at any time, and Junior particularly assured me that he had resolved to restitute his life, and make sure that he and Taku would be there for me more. He promised to get Taku a job at his new place of work, and of course did; and Taku was supposed to start the Monday after the Friday Junior left us. Even as I write this memoir now, I still want Taku to know that I could leave this world anytime, and if that were to happen, I would want him to be strong, courageous, and happy. I would want him to hold on to life as a believer, continuing to trust in the Lord and all around him—those he knows really do care about his well-being. I would want him to use whatever resources I would have left for him to improve upon his life and make himself comfortable. But of course, this didn't mean that I had any intentions of going anywhere anytime soon. Only God could determine our time here on earth.

It is appalling and devastating for any parent to have to walk into his child's room and find him or her unconscious or dying, as I did. How could I have spent all day at home with my boys and not be able to notice that one was dying in his room? Why did my parental instinct not lead me in there earlier to arrest the process and save him? Why did I not involve him to help Taku with the internet bed search when I passed to show him an ad? Did he decide to come spend his last days with Taku and me for a reason? Was the cancellation of a planned visit to Foin in Dumfries that day some signal I must have missed? Or was it just fate that held me back for things to happen the way they did? Should Gilbert have taken him with him to Silver Spring the night he said he visited him in Woodbridge? And why didn't he tell me he was going there or call me while there, so he and I would run some ideas? Did Junior know he was going to die on that day, or was he practically unable to call me or his brother to help him out of some abrupt distress? Or did he just decide to get some rest and then died in his sleep? I will never know what to make of all these conjectures or innuendos, and no insinuations can enlighten my thoughts productively right now. Emmanuel Kafain Mbeng Jr. was at times rambunctious and recalcitrant when he was forced into doing what he didn't want to do; he was always ready to express a logical excuse for something he did and would become cantankerous when he wanted to have it his way. But he was also condescending and very smart; he was coolheaded, proud, caring, funny, and loved life and dance, and sprinted on four-by-four relay just like his grandfather did on the one-mile races at the commonwealth games in Lagos in the forties. In spite all this, my son was also very worried about his mistakes—mistakes that most probably led him into some unconventional activities that he was definitely too scared or embarrassed to discuss with me.

And I know so how? I know so because he was my son. He told me some of his follies, but feared he would hurt my feelings with the more serious ones, which may be why I did not see this terrible outcome coming. I was quite certain at the Sentara Hospital, when his mother and I visited with him, that his normal senses had to have been compromised for him to address us the way he did. From the way he expressed himself and behaved, I knew I had a lot on my plate on restitution; but I wasn't aware of the gravity of his condition to be able to redeem him more. It is obviously too late to worry about all of this now, and I wish no one actually should. Yes, and I mean yes, my son liked schooling, but was distracted by some choices he made, and the people I guess he confided in might have failed to let him know he was drifting toward a wrong path; but they determined otherwise when they made ridiculous proclamations about his potentials. Many people were fond of him, and rightly so, for he was lovable and friendly; but he hated the fact that people did not understand his plight enough but wanted to give him advice that could not help him in whatever situation he had implicated himself in. He did not come to me often, because he knew about my unwillingness to compromise my values, to accommodate his demands, even when he realized that these demands were counterproductive and more damaging in the long run for his destitute. And all who knew me profoundly also had to know how I interacted with my children, without reason to discriminate on discipline or otherwise. I was actually insulted at such insinuation after a prejudicial miscalculation of intervention. My love for my boys was the greatness of my life, and everyone close to me could attest to that. When the realization of reality finally came my boy's way, time must have run out on all of us, leaving everyone with the grief of consequence.

A little hope had been restored on to Delphine, Taku, and me, when the emergency staff responded relatively fast and took over the resuscitation process. So the drive to the hospital was actually in high hopes, even though Taku and I drove behind the ambulance in shock and disbelief. That ten-minute drive will go down in our history as the longest drive we would ever have made. In his shock, Taku remained quiet, as he does most of the time, except when he and Junior were together doing their thing. So Taku told me, "People like to say I'm too quiet, as if I should be talking even when I have nothing to say. I didn't talk even to Junior all the time, but he was okay and understood me just like you do." That was a sweet comment from my boy, especially since many people were beginning to suggest that he and I needed professional counselling.

PAINFUL LOVE

My eyes were fixed on this legitimate bond, staring at the showers of pain drop from it. My ears heard a voice that sounded so distant and faint, but was so real and acquainted. My heart knew how so much it owned, but couldn't explain the cruel passion that cracked my neck from side to side. The ignorance wasn't ready for the time, but there was no one else to trust but me, so I secluded myself from all fantasies of glory, driving the bitterness of sudden pain into a lonely heart—that burned, and hurt, and stole away all pride in the ability to love and to cherish that love. The ashes of which are now left behind in undefined but painful memories, with wishes of the hope of a fantastic rejuvenation, blemishing from a heart so deeply wounded to blame. But still wanting for it to be the way it was, or should have been, fearing only to retire by saying "fare ye well" to the broken pieces left of him. And dreaming that open minds will feel the dream that was forever meant to be, but in a battle of lose without weapon, passion has been taken for granted by a sense of black humor, and by instinct, great pride is lost and will be buried in terrible fascination, bringing out a victory that shall always be wrong!

My son, Kafain Emmanuel Mbeng Jr. loved life abundantly and cared very much about family, particularly his brother and mother. He would do everything to ensure their security and comfort, even when he had little or no resources. I know because he used to use whatever I gave him to get them something, and I always had to stop him from buying me something out of nothing. While he was developing his true sense of responsibility, God had a different assignment waiting for him, and it is for this reason that we gather to wish him farewell as he leaves us to pick up this new role. We are definitely going to be saddened by his sudden or premature departure, and only so because we still don't understand how God operates. It is important though to understand that Junior went home peacefully and now abides peacefully in heaven. I gave him back to God many years ago and enjoyed the time God gave him to me here on earth. I can't wait to hear his side of the story whenever I finally join him in God's Kingdom. May God continue to give you all peace and understanding in this sojourn of life on earth while waiting for your own call.

THE THEORY OF RAISING CHILDREN

Just like all kids, my kids were confronted with life's challenges, even if their challenges were conventionally different in nature from most other challenges. A home is made of parents and children, and sometimes uncomfortable adjustments have to be made in the best interest of all in the home. Whenever that becomes the case, the focus on family strengths, merits, and progress need to remain paramount. Shenanigans will be shenanigans, and good values in pedagogy will be good values, no matter community distortions. How each parent raises and relates to their children should be their business, and their individual ways must never be misconstrued as negligence, incapacity, viciousness, etc. Even when parents disagree on systemic issues, their children need to take a back seat and be left out of the discussion. Expression of emotional setbacks can lead adolescent kids into behavioral difficulties, and on basis of speculation, and without any evidence to propound any theory here, my conviction is simply that my boy could have been fighting very hard to subdue feelings of depression that could have stemmed from our domestic readjustments. And all the concerned individuals around him would have failed to isolate him from realisms of such discrepancy. This is an assumption. I tried and failed, but never gave up. I just believed, and strongly too, that he was eventually going to outgrow such convictions, if they were present, just as he seemed to have done in our last productive talk with his brother present. My siblings and I grew up in a pool of privileges, and I wanted my kids to enjoy such privileges too; but the privileges I managed to provide them became inconsequential to the need of time, which could be how my actions could have ended up spoiling my son—I hope not! But his brother turned out okay, so spoiling them couldn't have been the case, and I am certain about this.

Kakwah, Nain, Fien, and I had just joined Joe, Brown, and family at SD's for a private convention dinner. And just before we sat down to be served, a text came in to me from Grace and changed every positive thought on my mind about further participation in what was left of that New York convention. Junior had been rushed to the hospital, and the picture was bleak. I wanted to leave immediately, but Kakwah went outside and had a talk with Grace, who said it was okay to stay the night and drive back in the morning, since things had been stabilized and were under control. Anger, fear, and despair were already building up inside me, and I was certain that the need to look deeper into Junior's life choices had become expedient, if we were going to rescue him from whatever melancholies he had gotten himself into. On occasion, his mother would complain about his midnight activities, but he would negate and try to persuade me that he was okay, claiming that his mom was just overly reacting when he was out late. So early that Sunday morning, Del and I took off from the Yonker Hilton, and I sped back nonstop to Alexandria. I picked up Taku, and we drove down to the Sentara Hospital that afternoon as he briefed me on the events of the previous day. We spent some time with Junior and were told he would be released the following day.

That day, Monday, I left work and rushed down to meet Grace at the hospital. She provided me with more updates, but this time, she and I experienced a different side of our boy. That was the last time the three of us were together, and that must be when we knew his problem was more deeply rooted than we thought. He was so belligerent in expressing himself to us, such that we both left the place so confused about what we needed to do next. That night, Junior called me and said he was coming back home to me; and of course, his room was always empty when he was gone—the choices to be away were always his. Taku was going to bring him home, but they stayed over in Woodbridge. Gilbert says he was down there, and that they had a great conversation, including his girlfriend, whom he says he met for the first time. Next day, Tuesday, he had appointments in Woodbridge/Dumfries. Then on Wednesday, Elsie brought him to the house in the evening. She said they had gone to have dinner to talk somewhere, and she had afterwards felt obliged to bring him to me. Could she too have known then that something tragic was about to happen? Was there some discussion in their circles that was providing her with unidentified clues? These questions I must ask! Strange things were beginning to happen, and vibes were beginning to surface, but no one could see into the future. While I was at work on Thursday, Junior called to ask if Taku could take him down to Woodbridge. I said yes, but also cautioned about an early return home. On that Friday morning, he said he came home late that night because he had stopped over to greet his mom. Was that also a final goodbye, and did he know that? Or should I have read more into that statement to ask more and keep an eye more?

I have a shrine at the entrance of my home in memory of my parents and sisters, which I stare at each time I pass by, and something kept dragging me to it weeks before my son would be called; but I never imagined in my wildest dreams that I would be adding a child to my shrine-wall.

LIFE WITHOUT MY SISTERS

Reflections on my sisters were prevalent on my mind all the time; and I always wished to have one more day with my immediate follower, Victorine, who had definitely wanted to talk with me before her untimely departure in Senegal in 1996. Joy had died in an accident on the terrible Victoria Bamenda road that went through East Cameroon; and Angeline and Irene all left me through illnesses, in 1998 and 2000, respectively. It was about six one morning when my phone rang; Ben was on the phone when I picked up. I had just returned from a meeting of our declaration of Southern Cameroons Independence, and he was anxious for updates. All I thought about then was Vicky, probably because our cousin, Hycenta, and I had sat on the same table all night chatting on their social indiscretions in high school. I knew I couldn't keep Ben waiting much longer, for anxiety could kill him. He was my secret confidant, and we needed to consult on the events of that night. So we agreed on a time to discuss details later on that evening when my head would be clearer. Even Rose had lost her abilities, becoming quite unproductive to Gilbert and myself, and all these melancholies were affecting my state of mind. We couldn't talk, we couldn't discuss and manage kids and family issues like we used to, and the bond that we had growing up as kids was lost and buried in terrible fascination, as I express in my poem, "Painful Love." Living without my sisters had left me empty, and always terribly frightened, so encapsulating what could have happened to my son was flabbergasting and obscure.

Ten weeks had gone by, and I still hadn't had word from the detective that was on the case. He had promised to call us with updates when they were available, and as dreadful as I may have been about learning why this happened, curiosity and closure were ripping me apart. I would occasionally pick on Taku's brain to measure his state of mind, and felt bad for him each time I cautiously tried to monitor his well-being. Not that I didn't trust his strength, but I feared becoming overbearing as I sort to ensure that nothing like what happened to his brother would ever happen to us again. Lamentation and constantly blaming myself, or others, was also not going to be helpful, neither to me nor to anyone that felt responsible for the plight; and no amount of "would haves and should haves" was going to bring Junior back to us. But not assuming blame wasn't also making me feel as good as many well-wishers wanted, and constant reflections of sadness ruled in my head all the time, especially when

I was home alone. That Friday and its remarkable course was never going to leave my memory no matter what. Which brings me to these possible theories:

1.   Did my boy overdose himself on something and was too scared to reach out to me and/or his brother for help? The three of us were home all day, none of us complaining of any anomalies, but for when he said his ears felt like he had just gotten off a plane. Would that have been seeking some kind of intervention without disclosing what he might have been going through? When he went into his room to rest/sleep, did he have any idea that he was doing so permanently? And if he had taken anything, would that have been by accident, or could it have been deliberate? And if deliberate, would there have been a reason why he would have chosen to end his life that way, mindful of the fact that he was surrounded by a loving family in every sense of the word?

2.   When Aunt Liz brought him home two days before after their private dinner talks, did she know he was on the verge of ending his life when she suggested his discriminatory frustrations and educational inaptitude? Or was it just some kind of practical joke that went bad? And would there be a logical way of getting answers to my hallucinations? Junior might still have died, or maybe not, but would his fate have been more admonishing or totally different on that day if he had not been taken to diner where x-ray on his life would be ascribed—probably injecting cause for more reflection on painful emotions in whatever indiscretions he had already been obliged to cultivate? Would this disaster have been averted if Uncle Vic had picked up my emergency call on that Wednesday that Junior was rushed home to me, two days before his tragedy? Vic was the lone relative of mine that knew every detail about my family's sanity—and more notably, the well-being of my boys. These remarks or rhetoric questions are, of course, typically subjective to specula-

tion, for the trip home was obviously an attempt to rescue and/or remedy some preconceived demonic characteristics that would have warranted such concerns. We will never know, nor understand why! But looking back at the bright side of things, his aunt might just have been destined for redemption from scrupulous embarrassment and esteem.

3. Listening to WTOP radio the other day, I heard a report by the National Suicide Prevention Center 1(800)2738655 stating that 67 percent of students commit suicide from depression, domestic and social problems, and educational difficulties, to mention only a few. There was a report on ABC News that funeral home directors say that a small amount of fentanyl can be very deadly, and such reports now raise my eyebrows. Even a caller said on the Howard Stern Show that he had lost his twenty-nine-year-old son to OPIODS, making me question myself even more. There is no doubt that these statistics got me wondering whether any of these issues had anything to do with my dear son, mindful of all the plethora of events that were beginning to feature in his daily life. We watch these reports on the 5:00 PM news every evening, but one never imagines it could be him or his son on breaking news, and yet there I was with my dear Taku, Del, and Grace, suddenly left to juxtapose on the anger of death or the denial that it had actually visited us.

4. JR had to have gotten himself wrapped up with the law and was probably so afraid of the outcome. His license had been suspended, which is why I didn't let him drive. I allowed Taku to drive him when it was absolutely necessary and restricted the drops to daytime and early evenings only. He and I were working on reinstating his license, and he had a lawyer representing him on this. He probably had other issues that he kept from me and refuted most of the concerns that his mother raised whenever she needed my rapid intervention. I know he was on probation, and maybe the fear of incarceration when he missed one appointment had

sent waves of panic into his head. He knew very well how I felt about breaking the law, and I'm sure he wanted to do well by me, but could have been cut short on time, if that's what actually happened. Whatever JR's state of mind, he was a strong and brave child, and had already shown me that he could handle lots of difficult situations. So I didn't think that after swimming across the ocean, hyperbolically speaking, he would drown in the sea. Our fights were usually about (1) his wearing of pants below his waist as was strangely becoming a norm for gangsters; (2) smoking any kind of smokes or narcotics in my house; and (3) bringing girls home, especially when no one was home to monitor their activities. These were normal fights in most households and couldn't have pushed him into any kind of depression. And of course, what could have happened to Divine Intervention that would let the son of a devout deacon become so repudiated from the goodness of life on earth? A rhetorical question on my mind at the time.

Whatever happened, happened because it was destined to happen, and this I have emphasized and reiterated over and over again to Taku and his mother since this ordeal happened. They knew him so well and would have stopped him, if only they had foreseen this consequence. We all are just stunned! September 7 was his birthday; it still is, and yes! We did celebrate it this year differently—without him. It was not a regular celebration, but a celebration of life nonetheless, as his mother, his brother, his sister, his uncle, his cousins and nephew, and I all gathered at his grave to retrospect and memorialize feelings of love—as painful as they were. And I have a feeling that he was there watching, and smiling, and wishing that we could understand that he was enjoying himself in heaven, and preparing to receive each one of us when our time would come. He probably knows who shall be next, maybe, but may not be allowed to tell us; for only God has control over his plan for us all here on earth.

CHAPTER TWO

BIOGRAPHY AND THE
VACUUM OF LOSS

The day was June 29, 2018, and my boys and I were home all day. Junior was two months away from his silver jubilee, while Taku was waiting patiently for his twenty-first. Minutes and hours went by, but none of us, at least not Taku and me, could see ahead to know what we will be facing when it was nightfall on that day. At approximately 8:15 PM, after not getting through to Junior by phone, I walked to his room only to find his unconscious body laying halfway and face-down on his bed. Our world would be turned upside down from then on, and would-haves, should-haves, and could-haves would become the norm of guilt in my immediate and extended family. Retrospections and reflections would then start, and the circumventions on Junior's life would gain forefront in all our lives, with wishes of a fantastic rejuvenation, blemishing from deeply wounded hearts, that would hurt, and pain, and steal away pride in our ability to rescue our son. And Junior's story, which began on September 7, 1993, would begin all over again.

Junior's father and mother were introduced when Rose, Prince's older sister, went down to Victoria for a Sakerette convention in 1992. His father and Aunt Judy had grown up as Baptist kids, attending religious youth camps together—the one to remember being the one in 1970 at the Kom Baptist Teachers College in Njinikijem, with Evan Schneider present. Judith and Rose were students in Saker Baptist

College, Victoria, and Prince went to Cameroon Protestant College, Bali. Many incommunicado years had gone by after the camps, but the name Judith Abong never vanished from Prince's memory. So when his sister mentioned that Grace was Judith's sister, no "chemistry" was needed to dilute the "solute and solvent" of their convenient love, as Victorine would later call it. It was automatic, and Kafain's American mother, Professor Eugenia Shanklin, a renowned anthropologist in Princeton University, New Jersey, became the catalyst in the equation that instantaneously developed the relationship into marriage and productivity. Their first meeting was actually at the JFK airport in New York; and their first drive to Alexandria in Virginia went through Princeton, where an informal engagement formality was initiated at the Shanklin residence. Even as far back as then, tragedy did not spare Kafain, for Joy, his junior sister, had just died in an accident on a return trip back to Bamenda from Victoria. She and Rose had gone down to visit Grace and her parents for a traditional "knock door" ceremony and were on their way back.

The rest of the drive from Princeton to Alexandria was smooth and romantic, and that evening at the Foinchases was remarkably eventful for all of us; Vic and Elsie and Grace and myself began to acquaint ourselves as the family unit that would come to be in the many years to come. Their wedding date would quickly be set before Grace's return to the Cameroons in June of that year, and Prince would then follow in November, obviously to make himself available for the occasion. That would be the first time Prince Kafain would be returning home since his departure, just to run into a state of emergency imposed by the government. Presidential elections had been rigged—as always was the case there—leaving behind total chaos in a country that absolutely lacked or always ignored the rule of law and order. Kafain and Vumah did however manage to wed in December at the Baptist Mission Center in Bamenda, with a fantastic reception at the Ayaba Hotel. Special permits had to be obtained and security officials hired—all to protect the wedding party from a very tense political atmosphere. Ni John Fru Ndi had won the elections, but the incumbent President, Paul Biya, refused to give up power; and this led to discontent and rebellion all over the Anglophone regions of the nation. Anglophones wanted justice and the restoration of their rights to self-governance, as was granted them in a 1961 Resolution of the UNGA. It was during these difficult times in the history of Southern Cameroons/Ambazonia that Junior's parents came together to start a family that has been so incomprehensibly altered.

Judith and Rose did not falter in their leadership roles throughout the ceremonies and meant only well in everything they did, being the matriarchs of both families that they were or needed to be to ensure essential peace and happiness. The discussions between Prince and Judy continued to reflect their religious teachings in those their youth camp seminars, and both never forgot that they had been growing up as sister and brother before becoming in laws.

Junior's parents: Vumah, Kafain, and Zaah; Junior's mothers, and Taku

Junior, Daddy, and Taku in Woodbridge; Junior's mother and brother

Junior was born to the Mbeng family in Detroit, Michigan, on September 7, 1993. Grace, Kakwah, and Nain had made this choice of Michigan in Bamenda, after Kakwah and Nain's wedding. I was still in Bamenda when Grace came back to Victoria with our baby boy. The news got to me from one of Grace's colleagues, a.k.a. Grace, who met Rose and me on our way to the Nkwen church. After the church service, my friend, Prossie Poufong (of late now), and I decided to run down to Ndop to inform my folks about the arrival of their grandson. Dad would later say that he carried a tin of oil and smoked meat to Babanki—as the tradition entailed—to formally announce the birth to Grace's parents in Babanki. I left for Victoria to go welcome my bundle of joy and was very excited to see him. We spent that first night enjoying each other's warmth, while his grandmother watched us. Grace and Georgette had gone to Bota for an all-night party, but that didn't bother me since I had my boy to keep me company.

After an extended stay in the Cameroons for our Bamenda wedding, I ran out of funds to be able to do things the way I was accustomed to, and this had a great impact on my personality and capabilities. Money commands respect and authority, and with little or no financial strengths at that time, my big sister, Helen, decided to put me in her Bastos residence in Yaounde—where I would comfortably hide, while waiting for my permanent resident visa interview date to mature. And because Grace was working and helping out with our boy, the pressure on financial responsibility became relatively bearable. I would make frequent trips to Victoria to see her—and be with our son, Junior, in particular—and couldn't wait to bring him back home to the States when all was set and done, where he would enjoy his citizenship rights of life. For some complicated family reasons, I wasn't allowed take him to my parents before leaving to come back, but I made up for this when both boys accompanied me to Belo many years later. The boys were actually very thrilled with the visit, and everyone was extremely happy to finally meet them. They would run around inside the rains, rub themselves in mud, and be followed around by local kids their age, who would be drawn to them by their American accent. Their grandmother made jokes about having to wash their clothes every day, for they changed clothes at least three to four times a day. They were free to go around and come as they wanted, with no security issues to worry about. I now wonder whether it could have been prudent for me to leave them there with my parents. Not so sure, and of course, Junior didn't die because he didn't have the appropriate attention. Grace and I gave it to him all the time, no matter what.

Junior and his mother had travelled to the Cameroons for an extended stay after his birth, and when they finally joined me in Annandale, Virginia, he also would join the ranks of Lambert, Becky, Victor, Nancy, Derrick, Mckenzie, Margaret, Raisa, Stephany, Vinielle, Melai, Emade, Visisibom, Tony, Jesse, Sandra, Chima, and many more. He also immediately gained notoriety, as the flamboyant jokester that he was. Life was very sweet for us as new parents in those days, and we cherished having all our kids around in all our gatherings. We spent weekends at each other's house, and lived as one big family—the Foinchases, the Tangs, the AchaMorfaws, the Njomos, the Chiatohs, the Juas, the Adamus, the Njimbongs, the Bretons, the Tansindas, the Yuhs, the Ayeahs, the Ndangas, the Ayunijams, the Ngembuses, not forgetting the Mbeng/Abongs, and so many others. And we were all always very happy together. It was amazing to see all these kids—who now were all grown into young adults—gather around Junior's remains, as they all bid him farewell on that July 14, 2018, day.

Junior went to kindergarten in PNEU Victoria, pre-school at Weyone in Annandale, grade school in Parklawn and Marshall, middle school in Benton and Potomac middle schools, and high school in Potomac High School. Then in 2010, he went to college at the Northern Virginia Community College. He used to say he had a child, PHD, because he had gone to very many different schools, one of his remarkable rokes. He was a good athlete and ran the 100-meter races like a Ben Johnson, reminding me of his grandfather in his days at the commonwealth games in Lagos. His friends and relatives all loved him a lot, and his love of music and dance moves featured special attractions. His little truancies got him unequivocal attention everywhere around in the neighborhood, and his absence at our "cir-

30

cle of friends events" was always highly noticeable and missed. When Taku joined him in 1998, he was so excited to have someone at home to play with and take care of, and he would do so, so well, becoming the big brother that Taku would come to cherish for all his life. Taku idolized him as a baby and wanted to be with him everywhere and all the time. In a way, I am glad that Taku was there with him when he went to final rest!

Unlike Taku, who is relatively quiet and does not demonstrate adolescent characteristics like his brother did, Junior was exceptionally assertive and would pass for a "show boy" anytime anywhere, never shying away from experiment. His mother and I often took robust measures to hold him back from one anomaly to the other and frustrated each time the conundrum was getting worse. No matter what, our love of him never fell short, which is why his death has left a vacuum, not only in our hearts, but in the hearts our entire family.

His remarkable speed in the hundred-meter races keeps reminding me of my dad's sprinting days when he too was about Junior's age in the thirties and forties or so, also reminding me of my shattered dream to bring him to the Olympics. But while we propose, only God can dispose! Watching my Junior carry his relay team from last place to first place when he crossed the finish line at the Northern Virginia Potomac High School trials remains my most—proud moment of his accomplishments, and all the compliments from his coaches and friends at Potomac High still echo in my head to this day. Every parent on the stands gave me the thumbs-up when they found out that I was his proud father, and one even told me that I had a potential Olympian in my house, if my son kept up with such speed. But Junior didn't, and even refused to take advantage of this adulation. Before I knew it, all his spikes were gone, and he refused to report for trials ever again. I was very disappointed, but relieved about all the travels that would have followed, had he continued to participate in those athletic events. Then he said he preferred basketball, but never made it through the selections, as the competition there was always more vigorous and challenging, with so many candidates always ahead of him.

Just like me, Junior loved music and dance, but unlike me, he wanted to make a career out of it and would tell me very little about his plans since his genre of music didn't even interest me to begin with. He was into the rap music, and I wasn't quite fond of it, especially the lyrics. My son was quite vocal, and this attribute always added value to our silence at home. He gave us something to talk about all the time, sometimes interesting subjects, and other times just argumentative issues, and he'd make his brother play and run around the house when he desired to just stay quiet somewhere in the house on his Xbox or something. Sometimes it was fulfilling, and at other times it was so annoying, but whatever the case, it kept the house warm and lovely, and you could tell how happy he felt doing it. He even remembered strange jokes from TV programs that he tumbled on, such as one which he said he heard on the Larry King show. And who would have thought he'd be interested on anything Larry King, but my boy was. The Larry King joke was about how we drive our cars on parkways but park our cars on driveways. That was funny to him, and he took time to explain this to his brother, who didn't get it at first. That was a great way to develop intellect, I thought to myself. I was always capitulated by the fact that he was average in most of his deliberations, but quite knowledgeable in his dexterity and antipathy for life.

ON CHRISTIANITY

"Can Taku have one too?" Junior asked me in 2008 when I told him that I wanted him to get baptized.

"Of course he can," I said. Sometime later on that day, I heard them chatting about this in the living room.

"Daddy is going to get me some baptism, and I'm sure you can get one too, if you want. Daddy said you could," he was telling his brother.

"What's baptism, and what does it taste like," Taku would ask innocently. He was just about ten then.

"It's like getting in a pool, only the church minister or some-body has to hold your hands and the back of your head, and dip you down and up," I heard my boy describing the process to his brother.

"Taku is too young to be baptized," their mother would chime in loudly from the kitchen.

"He'll not get any baptism now, and I'm not even ready for you too, Junior. You people must finish doctrine first, even though they don't have real Sunday School in that your church," she declared.

"But I'm above twelve, and Daddy says he and his best friend were baptized at twelve, and that Jesus Christ was twelve when He too was baptized," Jr. argued in his usual logical style. As an ordained deacon at Mount Vernon Baptist Church in Crystal City, Virginia, the church pastor, Rev. Martha Philips, had requested to baptize both my boys at the same time, regardless of their ages, because she knew them and our family very well.

"There is actually nothing wrong with baptizing children, especially when their parents are very involved in the church," Rev. Martha Philips said. "And the Catholics do it even at an earlier age because of the faith of the parents." It wasn't my desire to argue religious philosophy with a servant of the Lord, especially if I conceded no harm in what she was proposing, so I somehow talked Grace into letting go her own belief about readiness, so that we could give our children back to God as was required by the teachings and command of Jesus Christ.

The preparations for this day were quite challenging though, and Grace constantly changed her mind on the reception venue after the service. But in the goodness of the Lord, all ended well, and her emotions were visibly clear when the angels of the Lord descended, inspirationally, on that Sunday morning to put joy on all faces, and especially that of Grandma Amina. Aunty Petra, Uncle Kakwah, Aunty Elsie, Uncle Danny, and Uncle James were all godparents for these kids, and the reception that followed at Ma Rene's Place in College Park, Maryland, thanks to Uncle Felix Tang, was very tell-ing of the family connections that Junior and his brother had. I was pleased, and felt religiously accomplished, for giving back my chil-dren to God—a very special and unique ritual in all of Christianity.

But giving back my son to God in death was never a feature that I ever would have anticipated to this day.

With the deaths of most of my siblings and parents and other very close family members, death had always been painfully real to me, but it became more real now than ever when I was compelled to fight to control emotions from my incapacity to stop it from snatching my son away from my very own hands. It has been a bitter pill for my boy, Taku, and me to swallow. Uncle Emman (Dr. EML Chiabi) and Aunty Emma Yoti had just returned to Laurel from Spain and were already waiting for us when we got to the funeral home. I had requested for a private family visit with Junior—the first actual view of him since his ambulance ride to Mount Vernon Hospital. What a difficult moment for all of us! Seeing Junior's lifeless body was absolutely devastating to Grace and to me. Aunty Yoti wouldn't even dare to come in, and we all were broken-hearted. Grace tried to express her feelings in her rant, but her words understandably lacked coordination. What could she say under such crude circumstances anyway. I am not even sure that she realized she was talking or chanting, and neither did I know what I was saying, when I too spoke a few words to him. It was terrible seeing his mother in grief, and as I stood and held him, I said a silent prayer to God to save her and give us all the courage that we needed to pull through the difficult times ahead. And of course, God did just that! Our boy lay there in peace as if he was just sleeping, but there was no life in him, and it was certain to us that he was forever gone. Dominic, Joe, and maybe Gilbert took pictures, and I was glad that Taku had abstained. The stress would have been too much for a child, and that would have created an even bigger vacuum in his life.

I then started to initiate funeral plans immediately, not wanting to keep my son in the morgue and/or funeral home longer than would be necessary. I quickly summoned his mother and her sisters and Taku to the Fairfax Memorial Funeral Home to discuss the logistics, and then to the memorial park to acquire the burial plot and final resting place. We agreed on dates, and on July 14, 2018, barely two weeks after that dreadful day, Junior's life was celebrated by numerous mourners from all walks of life in our metropolitan community of family and friends. Everyone who had to be there was there, and the acceptance of his fate started becoming bearable at the reception hall, when we all tried to bury our spite and differences in order to memorialize only him from then on. There was good food coordinated by Georgette, Regina, Petra, Laura, and Delphine, and the speeches were perfect. The BOBANS, SAKERETTES, and WOINKOM, DC were all there, and sang their favorite alumni songs. Uncle Vic was master of ceremony and made sure that he had every angle covered for the farewell of his boy. I could tell he hated doing it, but who else would have taken charge than him.

My bosses, friends, and executive clients—Hons. Wayne and Lea Berman, President Rick and Diane Pollack, Mrs. Janet Davidson, Ms. Peggy Vasquez and her son and grandkids, and Ms. Shami Scott—had all come to pay their last respects at the viewing and funeral service/interment, respectively. This was huge recognition to my family, for we all had been raising our kids and grandkids at the same time and would update each other regularly on most, if not all, developments in their lives. They were all very touched by the news of Junior's passing when I called. Mrs. D, who had had her own fair share of tragedies from the deaths of Mike, her first son, and then Mr. Davidson, her husband, was completely devastated. She could relate on the nightmare of the loss of a child and wanted me to understand that I was not alone in the experience. Both Mr. and Mrs. Berman were flabbergasted when I told them I was sending Chris to take them to Dulles airport because Junior had died the night before. It sounded like a practical joke to Mr. Berman, and his brief silence on the phone was indicative of shock, especially when he heard my teary emotions. Mr. Pollack hugged me tight in front of the AHA office after our trip to HHS for his meeting with the secretary. I had waited to tell him after the meeting to be prudent. Darlene must have been wondering what I told him when tears literally ran down his face as he rejoined her at the entrance to the building. I was very disillusioned by everything that was happening around me at that time, but the show of love and concern was, at the same time, strengthening my zeal and thoughtfulness in handling the ordeal as a testament of my faith in the Lord. I also quickly remembered the Bible story of

Abraham and Isaac. I knew for sure that I was not going to be alone in the pain of it and pleaded with the Almighty's indulgence to my leadership role in the family.

Watching the vice president, Joe Biden, struggling to talk about the loss of his son, Bo Biden, on *The View*, a show on ABC Television, brought tears of emotions to my eyes, particularly when both he and cohost, Megan McCain, began to tear about their losses. I had met the Honorable John McCain several times before and knew about his greatness as a person. The VP, His Excellency Joe Biden, was emphasizing to Whoopi and her colleagues that "You've got to find a purpose in order to overcome the loss of a child"; and this he did with a teary eye. Again, this encapsulates the fact that it is extremely difficult to deal with the pain of the loss of dear one, even in celebrity circles. Fame and money does not ease the pain at all, and painful memories are always be rejuvenated whenever the subject of loss of a dear one comes up. The empathy demonstrated by the VEEP exemplified the camaraderie in which we live, and like he articulated so well, saying we know what anyone with such loss is going through is an understatement, for no one but you alone can say how you feel.

The support and kind words from friends and well-wishers didn't stop me from continuing to feel that I had failed to do something to avert my son's catastrophe. On October 10, while we drove from her home to DCA, Mrs. Berman told me never to feel guilty that I had not done enough, and this view would also be reiterated by Mr. Berman the next morning—as we drove and chatted on our way to the office. Before Mr. Pollack left town a week before, he had told me that the feeling of such lack of control over my plight was always going to be present with me every time I reflected on my son, he and advised that I remember only the good times we spent together, while focusing more on his brother's emotional sanity. I was already trying to do just that. So I promised to do so before we changed the subject, to discuss the hurricane forecast in the south. And despite all these attempts to distract me from reliving this ordeal, the big question about why and how this could have happened to me was permanently present on my mind everywhere I went. What did we or I miss, I constantly thought; and out of the blue, a huge vacuum had been created in the Prince Kafain family—causing us to continue to wonder whether or not we really have an understanding of life here on this Earth as we sometimes claim to do. My guess is that we just have to be content with what we have and not what we strive for, even in the optimum comfort of our hopes.

Junior and I shared a name: Emmanuel Kafain Mbeng. At his birth, I had suggested Paul—my late brother's name—to Grace and Kakwah, but Grace wanted Emmanuel, and of course, she won. That was okay too, and we were fine sharing the name when Junior was growing up. The echoes of "Emmanuel! Emmanuel! Go, Emmanuel!' when he ran or played football gave me the pride of being his father, and though we called him Junior at home and in our extended family, we all knew his name was Emmanuel, and we all used it in talking about specific things in relation to him. He owned the name more, since I had decided to use Prince Kafain in all fora. All his friends loved the name, and there was certainly something special about it even to him. "So many Emmanuels in my family," he would remark and ask why our family was so infatuated with the name Emmanuel. "Uncle Kakwah—Emmanuel, big uncle—Emmanuel, big uncle Professor Chia—Emmanuel, daddy—Emmanuel, me—Emmanuel, maybe you too should be Emmanuel, Taku," he would joke in his usual style when poking fun with Taku on how his name was less popular, even though Taku was named after great-grandpa. My boy used to find a way to make conversations exciting in our home, and in many ways, his absence now leaves a vacuum in our household that will be difficult to fill, particularly to his brother, whose ability to smile has faded away tremendously since that fateful night. My wish, hope, and prayer is for him to remember the good moments that he shared with his brother, and find a way of living happily again, for that certainly would be what Junior would want, and I know so.

Junior, Daddy, and Taku on
Father's Day 2018 in Fairfax

Kakwah, Grace, Gilbert, Nain,
and the Prince after JR's death

CHAPTER THREE

IMMEDIATE FAMILY REACTIONS

Of course, brothers Richard, Stephen, Zachs, Eric, and Sammy, and sisters Helen, Anna, Florence, Esther, and Rose were petrified and too dismayed to say anything. No doubt that they never thought they would ever be the ones consoling me for the loss of a child, and all seemed to be avoiding me when the news was still fresh. When I finally could speak to Helen, our oldest, I immediately had to hush her down when she attempted to insinuate and gravitate towards the blame game. That was one thing she had in common with both our mother and grandmother, and I wasn't ready to entertain any negative unproductive thoughts that would only increase the excruciating emotional pain that we were already dealing with. Blame was out of the picture as far as I was concerned, a perfect way, I believed, to unite, not divide, the family.

Queen and I grew up as besties in the sixties, and our mothers, Frida and Mary, were best friends (more like sisters). They raised us all like children from one family, and I was the lone boy in the midst of all the girls: Beri, Malai, Victorine, Love, Joy, Patricia, Felicia, Angeline, and Irene; and Sam and Gilbert would come in the later years. It must have been my loneliness as the only boy in the family that strengthened my bond with Joel (Roy), when his mother brought Charles and he got home from the Biafran war zone in 1966. When Junior died, I immediately called Roy, who had just left me a few weeks before, and I am sure he too called Love, who in turn called Queen. Queen was in London visiting with her daughter and didn't know what to do, nor how to talk to me about such a terrible subject; so she just decided to send me this religious message below:

> Beloved we praise God for another new day. Our text of meditation today is Psalms 27, and the title is Confidence over Anxiety/Fear. Psalms 27 is one of David's psalms. David surely wrote this psalms during one of the most trying times in life. We are not told which of these moments it was, but it was definite that the challenges were so great that David was anxious and afraid. In fact, in verse 10, David felt abandoned even by his own loved ones. In verse 12 he said "His false witnesses have risen against me and as such breathe out violence." But David chose to approach his anxiety and fear by looking up to God. He fixed his eyes on the Lord God. And when he did, he saw the Lord as his light and salvation."

At this point, I actually started enjoying Queen's use the Word of God to reduce my pain and anxiety, for I had always had an anxiety problem. And she continued:

> He saw him as his defense, and therefore, that overcame his anxiety and fear (verses 1–3). He confidently said, "though a host encamp against me, my heart will not fear. Though war arise against me, in spite of this I shall be confident." He concentrated on God, rather than the challenges. I asked of the Lord, that He might dwell in His house, all the days of his life. Be loved in moments like what we are currently going through; we naturally will be anxious and afraid. But the best way to overcome our worries and fears is not to blame Y or Z, but to focus on our

God. When David did this, he overcame his anxiety and fears. That is why verse 14 is very reas-
suring. The encouragement to you and I this day
is that we should focus on the Lord rather than
our challenges. [I was trying to do just that, but
doing so was challenging under the circumstance
of child loss.] If you focus on the challenges,
you can run into a deep pit, even when no one
is chasing after you. But if you fix your eyes on
the Lord, you will be courageous as David before
Goliath.

And then Queen ended with a simple "good morning." The
passage was quite reflective though, and whether or not she was the
composer, I appreciated it and made sure I told her when we spoke. I
also promised to share her religious thoughts in my subsequent story,
and she said, "Fine with me," so here you have it! It was certainly
inspiring, especially coming from a sister, whose sentiments always
meant a lot to me.

Malai reacted much differently. She had spent plenty of time
with Junior and Taku some years back when we visited her in her
Bojongo mansion in the Cameroons. She was absolutely speechless,
as Gil and I would expect, but managed in her ill health and grief to
make me understand that she was aware of what I was going through
and wished she could be present. She was silently tearing, and I could
hear Abongwa consoling her behind. She also invoked the Lord,
reminding me of how she and I grew up, and asking to know how
Taku, Grace, and Del were coping. Then she told me to tell them to
be strong, for it had happened again. I guess my sister was becoming
used to these occurrences in her family. I remembered her loss of
child in the early eighties, and the loss of all her younger sisters in the
score of years after. Until then, she had been a very strong woman
and the cornerstone of our family, and my parents relied on her a lot
in holding their family intact.

Love—and yes, I mean Love—cried and cried and called
Adenrele in Lagos several times, and then cried some more on the

phone. She found it extremely difficult to communicate her feelings to me, because she knew how painful the tragedy had to be on me, and she became very relieved when I told her that it wasn't anything that we all couldn't handle as believers in the destiny of the Lord. On Roy's part, he was plain angry and refused to socialize with his friends that whole week, which must have made them to realize how important our relationship really was. He had just been here in Washington for an educational conference, and Taku drove him around. He kept asking when Junior was coming to see him, and when he left, he said he was going to arrange to have the boys and me fly over to Nigeria, for the next Christmas "bash" at the Lagos compound. We were also going to go visit his Obudu ranch, he said, and he and I thought such visits would bring back whatever focus Junior was losing. Geoffrey secretly told me that all drinks were stale for him, and he hardly wanted to leave the house, except when he was going in to work. Our circle of friends in Abuja called me to share his grief and condole with me. Our kids were supposed to run our enterprises when we were retired, and retirement was just around the corner for us. It was very sad to us that Junior was gone, and we needed some reconfiguration.

Gilbert was lost for words. He was not speaking, and he and his wife, Laura, had immediately moved from their Silver Spring residence to my home in Alexandria, as would be expected during such times, and were now in control of activities in the residence as people were coming and going. Tears ran down my eyes each time I looked at how confused everyone seemed, and the wish to have been able to trade places with my son became even stronger and stronger. I had abundant pity for Taku and Delphine, who were there with me when our world seemed to have been shut down by an experience that we were never going to forget. I had quickly realized how strong they were and had only praises in my heart for them, also silently praying for God to give them all the strength that they would need in the days ahead. As the convention of people continued to flock in, I became more and more reminded that something was gravely wrong in my family. Occasionally, this was exacerbated by the fact that everyone was sympathetic towards us—even attempting counselling.

There was no doubt that the loss of my sisters and parents had been rejuvenated by the ordeal, for Gilbert was visibly deeply devastated when he passed by my memorial wall. His eyes remained bloodshot for a while, and we avoided eye contact as a way to prevent shedding tears with people around, but he still manage to go to Junior's room to overcome some of his emotions.

Kakwah had gone on travels and said he was sending Nain and Visi up for the funeral, if he didn't return before the funeral date. He had instructed Visi on what to do to alleviate my financial pressure, and I must remark here that Junior's passing was like a community affair. People did not just come; they brought drinks and made contributions to augment the big responsibility that awaited me. For that, I was grateful! My uncle JY Chiabi called several times to assure me that I was going to be okay when the mourning was over. He too had gone through the experience of the loss of child when Patience died in California many years before, and rightfully had the authority to instruct me on emotional dependency. He and I revisited the passing of Patience in Los Angeles, many miles away from him, and my emotions actually subsided when he described how he had felt then when Kakwah, Patrice, and I and Uncle Emman were dealing with travel logistics and funeral plans. She had been a "sweet flower" in our family—the Yuhs in particular—and she and I lived and enjoyed life in the States, exceptionally well. We were just two of us here from the Chiabi clan in the early eighties before Kakwah would subsequently join us, making life even better with the three of us sticking together as family. We didn't have cellphones as we do today, so communication was limited to landlines when we were at our individual homes. But something sinister surely did happen in our sister's life and stole her away from us. And now something sinister had just happened in our son's life and stolen him away from us too. Even Uncle SK 2 had some consoling words of wisdom when Dr. Chiabi made a phone connection. I was practically overwhelmed with all kinds of reactions from family and friends when Junior passed. Patrice and Valentine and their wives, Adeline and Michelle, and Kate and Larry, and Danny and Vivian, and everybody all gave me courage and moral support. Dr. Mike Leke and Jacob Waah all showed me love and special concern, and if anyone's name is absent, it is not because you have been forgotten, for everyone was significantly featured on my mind then and to this day.

I had bought some chairs from Walmart in anticipation of a big crowd for the wake, and Gilbert went back for more from his house. Throughout the days that followed, he took over fatherly leadership of Taku, Johnson, Evan, and Victoria and set the planning of the funeral activities in motion, in collaboration with Georgette, Laura, Delphine, and Petra, while Grace and I settled on a convenient date for everyone who could come. He would then come to me for the necessary funds. Generally, there was enough trepidation for Grace and me to feel about the unexpected loss of our boy. Grace and her siblings were also making funeral preparations from the Ngembus residence and were in touch with Gilbert and me to compare notes. Regina, Grace's twin sister, had taken over her sister's role as would be expected, and was obviously in consultation with Victor, I guess, as would have been culturally expedient. In my world, and by virtue of seniority and sanity, Regina was still their leader here, and she handled the role substantially well. She and I immediately cultivated a memorandum of understanding on the cooperation that was vital to erase retrospection of any past agony. And this understanding went so perfectly well that any pre-existing animosity became diminished by the peaceful and conducive mourning atmosphere that we created.

Dr. Joe Toyang had become very familiar with my phobias, anxieties, and mood swings from characteristics of depression and was already preparing some concoctions that would calm my nerves down, in the event that some unforeseen contingencies came up. Before my move from Springfield to Alexandria, Joe used to come down all the way from Columbia, sometimes in the middle of the night, to contain my migraine headaches or panic attacks that I often called to complain to him about on the phone. There was always a shenanigan or two that Junior or someone could have caused to upset me and give me these chills. He always rationalized and normalized the situation with his poised personality, and sometimes left me feeling so foolish for making him drive down sixty-plus miles just to come put a reasonable lid on some manageable scare. Joe minimized my reactions to my boy's braids, his pants below his waist, his smokes, his smart defenses on destructive ideas, and generally on his character dissolutions; and most importantly, he put a bridge for Junior to choose to cross, if he wanted and decided to. He said he knew Junior was going to realize and get out of these fits as he grew older, but that ended up not being the case. I could see and tell that Joe too was hurting badly from the pain of the loss, probably feeling that he could have done more to remedy the situation, especially after one of our unconscionable encounters in a Fairfax court hearing on a domestic and sensitive matter.

James Njimbong—a.k.a. Jimbo by me—had been there with me from day one of Junior's life. He usually didn't express himself about issues the way he should have, but he was dumbfounded when I told him straight to the point that Junior had died. I'm sure he did some private investigation about my announcement, when he said he was calling me back, and in his usual way, he avoided any discussions when he later arrived at my house, where family and friends were already gathering in numbers. Jimbo had sat my boys down in Springfield and told them that his only concern or interest in all that was happening in our family was their well-being and comfort. He was aware that Junior wanted to be where he could escape strict discipline, and even promised to pick them up anytime they wanted to stay over at his house with Melai, his son. He too was feeling guilty that he didn't see this coming and told me to be strong for he thought I had done my best. But my best had not been good enough, now that I was burying my child, who had in no way shown any signs of illness or distress.

It was so hard for Aunty Petra to imagine or believe that I was talking about Junior when I broke the news to her. She was my kids' godmother and aunt and was always there for them. "*Wetin you di talk so*," she exclaimed in lingua franca, and said she would call me right back. Either the news was too blunt and hard for her, or she wanted to call big brother Ben to draw some strength, since she was probably too shocked to immediately think straight. So a few minutes later when she could compose herself and call back, she rhetorically asked, "Which kind bad luck this?" in the same broken English. Our emotions were high and dominated by silence, and we quickly got off the phone. Petra immediately put on her direction hat and got in touch with Gilbert and the rest, and funeral strategy began—pending my decision on logistics. She had already called Joyce, who too was so devastated when she struggled to give me counsel on the need to hold strong. Her kind whispers of encouragement were significantly deep, and she said she just wanted to assure me that I would never be alone in dealing with such an emotional ordeal. "Mama is feeling so bad for you, and wants you to be strong and know that she is praying for you, and loves you," Joyce would say as her sweet voice faded away that day. I can't forget the looks on the faces of Ben Jua, Ngom Jua, Samoh Wallang, Funwi Ayunijam, Mike Bibum, Jacob Kona, Patrice Yuh, and everyone else; they all must have been wondering why such devastation would befall me, and where I could have mustered the courage to be dealing with it. Ben had driven up from Columbia, South Carolina, to comfort me, but looked like he needed more comfort himself when he felt the on-the-spot shock. There was no envy of anyone in my family, and when Taku and I broke down trying to make our farewell eulogy, Uncle Amos Mubang, Victor Foinchas, and some others in the family quickly rushed up to the stage to prevent any eventualities from our sad reactions. I would only come to know that we were surrounded with love from Christopher Chiatoh's videos and photographs. Valentine Chiabi, Martha Futsi Jam, and Kuof Foinbujof had also gathered all the kids around the open casket, and each one of them was trying to pass on some kind of a message to Junior, even if he wasn't able to see or hear them.

So many reactions from so many people! Felix Tang and his wife, Sheila were also so flabbergasted to hear that Junior has passed. Felix and I and my boys always spent time together when we lived in the Woodbridge/Dumfries area. He would occasionally make jokes about Junior's dancing skills, likening them to mine, and always suggested some productive programs he thought we should get the kids involved in. He was a true extended uncle to my sons, and he took care of them just like his own. He bought them little gifts and gave them pocket monies on occasion, and they knew he adored me from the day he arranged their baptism reception at Ma Rene's place in

College Park, Maryland. He didn't just know how he could be telling me "sorry for your loss," like people were saying, and told me the loss was his too. Of course, I knew just how painful it was on him and replicated similar sentiments to Danny AchaMorfaw, who had come with Ni Emma and Sister Julia—our doctor sister.

Danny and Bill Adamu were very concerned about events, and Danny made sure he informed most in our circle of friends, particularly JJ Waah, who came down all the way from Boston to help out in his very kind and special way. Dr. Michael Leke did same, driving up all the way from Fayetteville, North Carolina, with Olive to join us at the funeral. Christmas Ebini and I had been planning to go to a Southern Cameroons movie premier, and he was lost in thought when my excuse was that my son had passed away the night before our plan movie trip. "Stop this your jokes," he said as if he thought my story was going to change, and the tears and cracks in my speech left him too speechless. When he and Judith came over, he wanted details, but accepted to wait for a more appropriate time in the future. "As an outstanding and influential member of this community, you have to educate people on what to expect when we raise children under various difficult circumstances," my friend said as they retired to Landover, Maryland, that evening. That would be the first encouragement for the start of this manuscript.

One uncle who knew it all, but had no courage of thought nor action when this ordeal happened, was Uncle Victor Foinchas. That was where the boys and I would have been, had I not cancelled the trip down to Dumfries a couple of hours before calling him to cry out that Junior had died. He still hasn't found the courage to express himself about all the hypothesis, speculations, and innuendos, for to him, Junior's passing is personal and painfully irritating. He had significant involvement over Junior from birth and would give any-thing to have sanity for our kids, and in his abyss style, which only I would sometimes be able to read and interpret, he felt obliged if anything beheld my family. His familiarity with all my personal pre-dicaments was obvious and well-known by all in our community of friends and family, which must be why he immediately became elusive and unconditioned for the days ahead. I am positively sure that he would have told me if he knew anything about Junior that could have caused or led to his death. I decided to leave him alone though—knowing exactly what he was thinking and where his loyalties were. But one thing was clear: he had lost a nephew senselessly, and the fact that he didn't foresee it to avert it must have been, or still is, the number one chill that he has to deal with now. Yes, I joked with him on a concept of a knocked engine, and he and I laughed at my embellishment of the situation, not knowing how impacted we were going to be affected by my expensive joke.

Eziah AK and Liz Monju arrived three-plus months later, and immediately called to greet from Silver Spring, where they were to attend some wedding ceremonies. In my usual style, I played down the impression of emotional pain to allow them enjoy their object of visitation, but monitored Eziah each time we spoke to see if she would muster the courage to bring up my ordeal in remorse, sympathy, and/or even grief. And could see that she was visibly struggling with words of consolation, not knowing which would be good enough, and even more so because she knew whatever she said would mean a lot to me. We managed to get by during the few times we spoke or visited, and the day to their planned departure date, I raised the subject as we chatted and could tell that she and Elsie were glad I did. Ali Sule was present and tried to relate it to his plight from his losses of Major, Binta, Amadu, Amina, and Seydou, but my case was just a little more delated since I had now added a child to my siblings and parents.

Elsie explained how their dad passed in London, and I revived Raymond's memories and spiced it with humor and fun times I had with him. I told them that Raymond would have loved to be at Junior's funeral. He definitely would have wanted the position of chief protocol or coordinator in chief and would certainly have been calling and visiting with me, often and occasionally, just to ensure that I was okay. That was Raymond; I liked him, and he knew how to be passionate with his friends and family. Philip Ngundam must have believed Raymond and I were closer, when he insinuated and reminded me years after Raymond's passing, that he was my new and only "Dah" left. We used to call Raymond "Dah," but only a few of us knew why.

I too didn't know how to bring up Felix, a.k.a. Jerry, for condolence discussion—a disturbing loss to Anne—and I could tell when I left her with Ali that she was seemingly uneasy, especially since it was my decision to inform and call him over in the first place. So my curiosity about all that Ali had said to persuade me, and then facilitate the visit, had to wait till when I would learn the real facts someday, if that became really necessary. When I called to check on the safety of their flight, Eziah told me all was fine, even though Elsie's phone got misplaced or missing, and finally gave me her words of wisdom to remain strong, realizing that there was nothing I could now do to change the facts. I liked when she said I will see him again when God decides to call me too, and this piece of truth inspired my hope and thinking—that my boy was not dead but living in a new home in heaven, where we all will be someday, if we believe and do what God wants us to be doing.

Dealing with Junior's departure after all these reactions from loved and concerned ones made the reality of his death somehow acceptable, but the difficulty of understanding why this befell me was still too hard to swallow. The "how it happened" had just gotten more enlightenment when the funeral home called Grace with the toxicology report, and as certain as we now were that it was fentanyl that was cause of death, the painful emotions were once more rejuvenated when his mother called me in tears. I told her bluntly that it was good to know why our son had died, but also emphasized the need to remain calm and continue the closure process, as nothing could now happen to reverse the situation. Taku came in to talk to me too, and I reiterated the same message to him, wanting him to focus on his life forward. "Junior is always going to be part of our lives," I told him, "and we must continue to reflect on his life, only as a living experience." Taku has been exceptionally understanding on this subject, and I pray to God every day to give him all the resources and wisdom that he needs to endure the pain of this great loss. I may never be able to rationalize how, or why, Junior ended up with this horrific narcotic, but since the choice to not do so was there, and he chose to do it anyway, I won't allow his brother and mother continue to lament over an uncontrollable ordeal. They won't have to put their lives on hold but will try as much as they can to move in acceptance that it is all over with Junior.

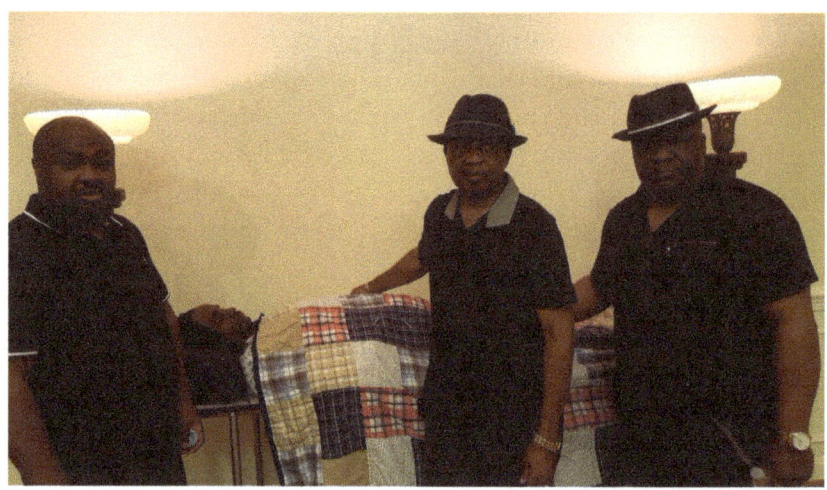

Uncle Emman, Kafain, and Gilbert in desolation

Roy and Kafain and Daddy and Taku in closure

Lambert, Becky, Junior, and Taku; Aunty Delphine and Junior

 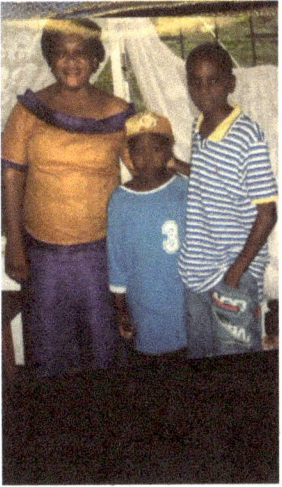

Mbeng kids and grandkids; Aunty Rose, Taku, and Junior

CONSTANT FEARS AND PARENTAL AWARENESS

I had just been shellacked in the field of childbearing, and the synergy with which I was now going to be addressing pertinent issues in my family obviously needed to be obliterated from my mindset. How to do so was a difficult task that gave me chills as time went by. I was constantly afraid; either that something would be happening to me, or to Taku, or to Delphine, or to Grace, Gilbert, and Kakwah, or even to some close family member at home or abroad; something that would make me relive the pain and the sadness of loss all over again and again. So the assertion that I had become afraid of life and its awakenings would be an understatement. My son, Taku, was very aware of this new me and would show pity in his reflexes, each time I seemed to be exhibiting emotions of fear. He knew very well that my constant trips to his room were obviously as a result of my fears, and he was absolutely understanding on one day, when I almost lost my breath because he was deep asleep and didn't hear me calling him to get ready and leave for school. Each time he failed to answer his phone while in his room, I immediately panicked and rushed in to see if he was okay.

Having children and being afraid that something bad would happen to them is normal and common in all societies. Whether they are babies, toddlers, or even adolescents and grown-ups, as parents, we develop all kinds of worries and fears of the unknown. We fear that something will hit them when they are playing, we fear that they could choke when they are eating, we fear that they will fall when they are walking, and so on; but we never really fear that they will not wake up when they are sleeping. Most parents like to know that their kids are sleeping, and during this time, some even seize the advantage to do some chores or make some phone calls. This is supposed to be the safest time for kids at home. So when a child dies in his or her sleep as mine did, fear becomes constant in most, if not all, aspects of livelihood in the house. You become afraid when your child stays too long in the bathroom, and even when you go to shower, you become afraid that something could happen to you in there and no one would quickly notice. Little things like that.

The absence of noise in the house was always unusual when my boys, Junior and Taku, were kids, and the statement holds true for most parents, even when their kids become adolescents. When my boys ran around the house, playing, shouting, yelling, and throwing things all over the place; my fear was usually always that they could hurt themselves in the process. And then when they finally got tired and passed out on either the carpet, chair, bed, or somewhere safe, I would just be happy to finally get a break from the concentration on them, to enjoy some quiet. The same went for their mother, who'd by this time have lost her voice from yelling out reprimands. And this cycle was routine daily, and no parent that I knew had a recipe to escape this phenomenon. Uncle Victor had the patience and was the best at handling all the kids when we got together, and Uncle Njabu's solution was for us to take them out and distract them with some junk food. The food at home had all the right ingredients, but didn't have the calming effects like the chemicals in McDonalds, Burger King, Popeye's, etc. This was what we thought, maybe just as a convenient disciplinary measure. Nonetheless, we, as parents, enjoyed every moment of it, including even the complaining; and at other times, we would watch movies with them on Uncle Vic's big-screen TV or take them downstairs to the basement in any of our houses to make them listen and dance to some music. We also made frequent trips to amusement parks, like Kings Dominion, many local centers, and malls in our neighborhoods. Again, and again, this cycle would continue over and over again, as our kids grew older and became more responsible and disciplined. We considered Becky as their young mother despite her age, for she'd always be struggling to carry Taku or some other younger kid around. Keeping them in base helped to reduce our fears and supervision. This cycle would finally end when all the kids graduated from high schools and colleges, but a new cycle of worries would take over—this time so unpredictable that all we as parents could do would be to worry a little bit more about our new predicaments.

At this developmental stage in their lives, they formed personal beliefs about aspects of life and had their opinions on how they preferred to handle decisions that would impact their lives. Malapropisms would become a specific concern for us parents, as a determination by the opinionated kids to fight hard on retaining their subjectivity and independence would immediately kick in. Most obedient kids at the early adult age would seek consultation from their parents before executing their desires, but kids who depend on peer pressures would continue to be cantankerous and silly and would rather listen to friends and others with very little to offer and always end up where they don't want to be. Some would realize this mistake early enough to make a U-turn, but some would spend more time than necessary and only come home when things get really bad. That must be a concept similar to that of the prodigal son in the Bible. Parents are always forgiving and ready to embrace their kids unconditionally, but sometimes even the parents miss the signals, and then end up more dissolute than at any time before. Some television programs and video games do more harm than good, even when that is not the production's intent. Such programing would only exacerbate they situation and drive parents even more furious and crazy when they run into arguments with their kids. This situation continues to worsen when parents try to impose ultimatums. Rules and guidelines for children to follow are good and always helpful, but must be applied with caution, so that they don't backfire. When children start breaking rules, they easily become stubborn, and rambunctiousness is not what any parent is looking for in bringing up their kids. It is important for parents to always guard against peer pressures, for most behavioral traits develop as a result of our children wanting to be like their peers, and some do so without evaluating the values of the attractions they are trying to emulate.

The noises that Junior and Taku used to make at home when they were in their teens was now completely gone, such that their presence at home was sometimes difficult to tell. Sometimes, they would even be watching TV without the sound, and I only later discovered that they were using earplugs. There was never the need to go in to their rooms only to check on them, for they'd say they were not kids and needed their privacy. Junior came and went as he pleased and hated my remarks on his late returns. He would cantankerously reject any effort I made to inject discipline, claiming he was not a kid and could take care of himself. Now I wish I had fought him more on this. Because he had breached my trust in his self-discipline, I became very worried and sometimes confused; and because I believed that with time, he would outgrow his obnoxiousness, I stopped harassing him about his choices and movements. Again, I now wish I had fought harder even though my success would have had to depend on what I specifically knew I was fighting against. He was still very compassionate though, and actually showed no signs that something was gravely wrong when he was with me. Instead, he would try to be the parent, asking me all the questions, and trying to direct me on how to stay emotionally stable and protected from "all the dangerous people out there," in his words. I often said he was full of shenanigans, and he would ask that I explain what I meant by "shenanigans." I prayed to the Lord every day that He help my boy grow out of his rambunctiousness, and positive outcome was beginning to be realized when he on his own volition told me that he wanted to build a good life for him and his brother. He had initiated an interview for Taku at the place where he worked, and on Father's Day, both of them decided to take me to a fabulous Tyson's Corner All You Can Eat, where we spent quite some time dinning and chatting on productive measures for our family. That really made me feel good to discuss with them as equals, and a compromise was reached on reinstating his driver's license, so he would settle back home without having to depend on rides from left and right. And this was barely two weeks before I would find him dead in his room.

While I was still trying to reflect on possible signals that we could have missed, Kakwah arranged a family gathering in Atlanta, Georgia, to sensitize a new spirit of togetherness in the Taku Chiabi family.

Chiabi grand and great-grandchildren at the 2018 Atlanta reunion

Larry and Kate had cancelled their trip to Canada to be present, and Kombem and Manigha had actually arrived a day earlier. Patrice and Adeline, Gilbert and Laura, and Delphine and I, and all the numerous kids from all our different homes convened at the Renaissance Hotel, ready to convoy over to the Kakwah and Nain residence. I haven't forgotten Hope and Kuoh, who were already at the residence making sure that the food was warmly sufficient. And of course the food was great, and well set up in a decorated basement, with huge Chiakuchia signs to commemorate the festivities. The uniqueness of the Chiabi clan was a shared feeling, visibly noticed by lovely interactions, unlike any time before. Someone, I don't remember who, made a remark that it was unusually strange to not hear the voices of Ka and Ka in a yelling mode; and that must have summed up the love and peace in the atmosphere. At some point, we all took numbers to talk to Uncle JY—the now-dean of the Chiabi family. We also took time to remember our youngest uncle, Uncle Henry Ndichia Chiabi (a.k.a. Simple Bodson—as he loved to be called), who had just died and was awaiting burial at the end of that month. The evening was punctuated by drinks, drinks, and more drinks, and interludes of a variety of dancing music that got all shoes off the feet of the girls. They actually enjoyed themselves from what I could see.

The next day, Friday, was even more remarkable. We had a delicious breakfast treat in a hospitality room at the hotel, and then everyone jumped onto a hired bus to go tour the Coca-Cola factory in downtown Atlanta. I am sure we all will be talking of this fantastic experience for many years to come, especially the production theatrics at the 4D theatre, where a high-tech demonstration of Coca-Cola and its magnificent productions of cinema and motion was spectacularly enhanced, to keep every visitor marveled at the brilliance of creativity.

That Friday afternoon was free or open to individual discrepancies. Some of us went shopping, some, like Ka, Larry, Patrice, Gilbert, and I, went back to Ka's complimentary suite for champagne; some, particularly the kids, went to the movies; and most others just rested or studied in their chambers or rooms—everyone just anxiously waiting for the evening's white dress code ceremony. We again gathered at the Yuhs for the main event, this time including some invited guests. Prince Kafain, the most senior member in the house, threw more enlightenment on the Chiabi family tree. Junior was again memorialized, and this time, in an extremely emotional big way. Kakwah had to speak after Prince, but the retrospective memories of his nephew consumed him so deeply that he became flabbergasted and emotionally speechless for a few minutes. There would be absolute silence in the room, with tears were running down many faces. Delphine quickly seized the moment to spiritually invoke and bring our united pain to God in prayer. And she did so, so perfectly well and so timely, that even Kakwah was now able to loosen up and continue his remarks and advice. He described Junior's birth in Detroit, granting credit to Nain and Grace for having made it easy on him. Adeline Viyoh would arrive then too, and we all quickly organized a welcoming toast for her, with Manigha speaking on our behalf. Dancing, drinking, and munching continued, and happiness was instilled in all of us like never before. I then nominated Kate and Manigha to enlist everyone, especially the children, for a savings venture, invoking JJC's financial delight, as I knew it; and Washington DMV was then proclaimed the next venue for 2019 reunion.

Going back to my constant fears and parental awareness on the subject of loss of child, there is a distinct difficulty in identifying signals of any behavior that would arouse concern and fear when dealing with your kids. This is especially true when these kids become adults and have independent minds on their own bones to chew. However, all the uncertainties that stimulate parental awareness must be looked into from many angles, as no one case is exactly the same as the other.

CHAPTER FIVE

SIGNALS AND ADVICE ON PREVENTIVE MEASURES

In my last book, *CANCER DIAGNOSIS IS NOT A DEATH SENTENCE*, I did clearly express there that my worst fear when I received my cancer diagnosis was to have to leave my boys, who were still very young then, to fend for themselves without a father. Little did I know that that wasn't actually going to remain my worst fear. I had now just buried one of my two boys, and the natural fear about retaining the one left was becoming my worst fear. I now saw that I had many worst fears. I was very afraid of how my boy would be able to handle my own death, if it suddenly came upon him. And how to prepare him for such eventuality was not easy at all, especially since I had thought I was preparing them both on that last Father's Day. I was also very scared that he, too, could be snatched away from me, so senselessly or stringently. So watching everything he did closely became my new norm.

There is a saying that "experience is the best teacher," which I believe is an understatement. My father lost a son in 1953, and another one in 1964. He lost four daughters in 1992, 1996, 1998, and 2000, respectively. But his experience wasn't enough to ease the pain. I can't say how long he would have had to deal with the pain of losing Daniel in '53, nor pretend to know how he felt in '64 when he left me in Buea to rush up to CBM Bamenda to bury Paul. And I would be lying if I claim to understand how he felt burying Joy, Victorine, Angeline, and Irene twenty-five years before he too gave up the ghost. The nightmare of the loss of child had to have lived in him throughout his life. Of course, the expression of this sentiment about my dad on the loss of child fully reverberates on my mother too. She bore us and must have been devastated when all these children left her in despair of death. While Dad dealt quietly with his painful emotions, Mum expressed her sadness in speech, saying whatever she needed to say to make her feel good and consoled. Rose and I were like Dad and Mum in that order, but I chose writing as my medium of expression, rather than speaking about things like our mother.

They say, "An apple doesn't fall far from the tree," and some say, "Like father like son." Sometimes these idioms are meaningful, when we examine the things that happen in our lives. My sister Rose lost a child in 1981 when I was working in Douala. The news had been delivered to me in the night, and I couldn't wait to leave at dawn to go be with her. Seeing me broke her even more, so I know exactly how she felt when the news about Junior reached her. I was with my boss on Capitol Hill when Gilbert called me in 1998 about Angeline. That too was terrible to hear, so I immediately decided that it was time for me to go home and redeem my family, even though I did not know how I was going to do that. Tragedy had become a norm in the Mbeng family, and there were little gossips here and there about what people thought was going wrong. Some, especially the church minister, said it was punishment from God because my dad would not leave the National Baptist Convention to join the Local Baptist Church, which had decided to break off from the main institution.

My family's plight could not have been a result of any of that, and I knew it, and even had to send away Mr. Peter Esoka, a renown Cameroonian journalist, who had shown up to our compound to interview my dad while I was there. "My family is mourning, and this is not a good time to seek to talk to my old man about church politics," I politely told him.

My dad had just finished reading the book of Job in the Bible, and gave me his Bible to read too, saying, "God does not give up on us when we believe in Him, even when we get tested, as Job was in the scriptures. You stay strong for your family, and that is just what I am doing. It is God that has brought you from the States to see for yourself all these troubles, and when you are finished, God will take you back safely." Wonderful words from a wonderful and brave man. I still miss his wisdom and eloquent speech to this day.

Wishing to prevent tragedy is evidence that one anticipates that tragedy could come. But most of the time, we are often caught with our pants down because of no warning signals. When the tragedy of loss of child hits you, you begin, on a daily basis, to seek reasons to find rational answers even when you know that the cause of your misfortune might just be the result of destiny or the will of God. To satisfy public opinion and curiosity, you try very hard to arrive at reasons that could have prevented your plight from happening, and sometimes this comes just to please anxiety caused by other sympathizers. When the cause of sudden death results from some kind of illness, the situation is generally more manageable, and preparatory measures are usually implored to overcome any resulting compromising emotions. I wish to offer below a little advice on some signals and/or preventive measures that are generally recommended when confronted with the dilemma of child discipline lest it leads to emotional catastrophe. Without sounding overly nefarious in my attempt to analyze some of these behavioral aspects of child pedagogy, it is prudent to state any characteristics with judicious integrity.

Let's look at some causes of behavioral disorders: namely ODD—oppositional defiant disorder, CD—conduct disorder, and ADHD—attention deficit hyperactivity disorder. All these causes have similarities in child or adolescent behavior, are time consuming. and are difficult to diagnose. Dealing with them requires a lot of patience and understanding from parents, for they are far more likely than clinical disorders to cause temporal behavior and/or emotional problems.

It is important to consider what parenting style parents need to implore, as some of these styles rarely carry the blame: (1) uninvolved parenting is a style that lets the child do what he or she pleases, with no rules and very little interaction, and this style is actually a show of neglect and should not be practiced; (2) authoritarian parenting is a style that promotes strict rules and no compromise and is usually one of the worst ways of dealing with disciplinary measures, and I definitely don't recommend it; (3) permissive parenting, which allows few rules and very little discipline, with no friendly role with the child, is also not a very appropriate style, for it cuts off much of the dependency on a parent for successful growth; (4) the parenting style which I highly recommend is the authoritative parenting style, in which the parent sets up strict rules, but has the willingness to listen and cooperate with the child on pertinent issues. Parents must learn to be patient with their children. Empathy, a cooperative attitude, and a calm temperament are very crucial traits or attributes for parents to adopt on the struggle to contain any abnormal behavior, particularly if violence is consequential. In extreme cases, professional help must be sort out. My son definitely did not possess any concerting traits, but most of us in our community of friends and relatives often implement a parenting style that focuses mainly on our cultural egos. The pragmatism of the society in which we raise our children will occasionally become underrated, and sometimes this helps to confuse the children, whenever they face the consolidation of their permanent personality choices.

"Children are very good at believing information that they receive from their parents," brother Sammy Ambe once told me in one of our pedagogic discussions with my dad before he left us. "So before you tell them anything, and I mean anything," he emphasized, "you must make sure you have all your facts straight and absolute, and be prepared to withstand any consequences." This interesting time with Sammy and Dad had occurred shortly after my mom passed in the summer of 2012. I had spent Christmas holidays of that year in Abuja and Lagos, without seeking Dad's consent as he would have desired, and while there, I had called to check on him and the rest of the family. He scolded me so hard for leaving the children in the States without proper supervision. I wasn't sure what he was talking about, but listened anyway, and then learned from him, and that same day from Kakwah, that Gilbert had lost all his property in a house fire. Dad thought it was irresponsible of me to not know the details, but quickly realized that I could only know something if I had been told. In the same light of parenting, he still expressed surprise that such devastating news was not given to me immediately, and was also shocked when I told him that I had been told to "just enjoy myself" when I heard and called them to check. To this day, I still can't say what actually caused the fire in my brother's apartment that almost consumed everyone in his family, and still remember like today how devastated I found them on my return home from abroad.

I can't stop imagining what a nightmare the outcome could have been to me and my entire family, and these thoughts were rejuvenated on both Gilbert and my mind as he drove me around during Junior's funeral arrangements and interment. He is still devastated as I speak and has obviously adopted the authoritative parenting style that he knows I recommend. Both Sammy and I understood Dad's frustration then, and Sammy coached me on Dad's dependency on me as the trusted patriarch of his family, particularly when he would be gone. That would be the only reason why he would grill me on something he knew I knew nothing about. In a very simple way, he knew how to discipline me, and said he did so knowing fully well that I had grown into a responsible man, who was now taking care of everyone in his family, including even him, which was all he could have asked God for. But he always added that as long as he lived, he was going to continue advising me as a child, even if his advice was inferior to my superior experience in life abroad or in general. "That is the parenting style I want you to teach all these children, and I'll continue offering conventional wisdom to the children I have left, until God decides to call me home to reunite with those that were taken away from me," Dad concluded in his usual soft-spoken tone.

We as parents are faced with assorted difficulties of handling our kids and their choices, and this happens each and every day, for each and every parent, and for each and every choice that they have to make. Saying that we as parents can tell them what to do all the time is an overstatement. We just need to be there for them, even when they make silly decisions and do things that we don't agree with. That said, every devoted parent would feel like a wimp or big loser if someone, and I mean anyone, inserted themselves and insinuated that they knew and understood your child more than you do. As you raise these children, you constantly try to implore only the best preventive measures on their discipline, on their development, on their economic stability, and on all character and moral values that will give you comfort about their integration into society.

As time went by, I had time to continue to reflect on how I ended up becoming a statistic, as seen on the evening news, and reflections on my faith in the Word of God were also significantly present all the time. I thought about how Jesus Christ, son of God, called all his disciples to have a last supper with them, and wondered why and how Junior's last meal at some restaurant didn't include me and Taku, or even his mother and sister, to secure that last memory and semblance of family biology. Listening to those crude insensitive but honest and from-the-heart remarks after his last trip to dinner was a challenge to my integrity and a compromise to my sanctity; and this fostered a reason for me to revive my determination to seek preventive retribution for me and my family.

WHAT PREVENTIVE MEASURES COULD I IMMEDIATELY THINK OF?

1. There are all kinds of signals that lead to all kinds of preventive measures: after our sad emotional and frightening visit with our son at the hospital, his mother and I had agreed on immediate action to restore his sanity when he was discharged. I then left her with some funds for food for the next few days, hoping that by that weekend, we would be able to start figuring out what we needed to do to remedy and salvage the condition. But money could then only buy food and not time, and I am prepared to accept that it was my fate, rather than the decision to interview him, move him around, and bring darkness to a story that he now owns, taking away my authority and opportunity to activate my action or contingency plan. A simple phone call might have savored this moment and made me feel better than I do now.

    I had just visited a CVS pharmacy to pick up some season's greeting cards for my clients and stood on the checkout line alone for more than five minutes, while a young man with a hoody sat and watched me from about ten feet away. Probably seeing me from his office video, the manager came out and told this cashier, whom I had thought was a customer too, to put down his hoody and help me. Interesting! For some strange reason, he immediately reminded me of Junior. It must have been the hoody. I paid for my cards and gave the young man some lunch money. I also gave him a brief lecture on the hoody, pointing out why it had become a dangerous stereotype for children of color in particular. Then I took a few minutes to explain to him why young people his age are often misconstrued when they hide under a hoody, while walking, driving, or even sitting at work with one on. It must be a new-age thing, for I had fights with Junior on this all the time, and still occasionally struggle to eradicate the hoody-culture with my boy, Taku, when he forgets to put his down inside a building or in his car. Many innocent children have been accidentally shot, and some killed, just because law enforcement couldn't easily identify them to be able to ensure even their safety; and I wish I could know how my reaction at CVS ended up impacting that young man. Educating our kids on the good values of life cannot be ignored or overemphasized in this day and age. Educating our children on the practicality of their behavior is an aspect of parenting that must not be underestimated. Sometimes we presume that these kids are knowledgeable, but some know only enough to get themselves in trouble; and then they sometimes learn only when time is almost running out. Being proactive on child delinquency is a parental duty, and no parent can be left behind.

2. Having friends is very important to kids. It is equally important to parents. Having friends with negative influences is the problem, and precaution has to be taken to ensure that our kids meet the right friends. "Show me your friends and I'll tell you who you are" is a statement that I

often hear some psychologists make, and I am sure they have conducted many studies on this to be able to make the claim that there is always some identical behavioral characteristics in friendships. Another common statement on this is "birds of the same feathers flock together." Children wish to act like their friends, dress like their friends, speak like their friends, and just be like their friends; and they often forget to take into consideration the fact that the circumstances under which they are raised sometimes differs from home to home, and for many different and obvious reasons. Some have a very good and patient understanding of this fact, but some give a damn to the consequences and carry on as they please. I was a victim of this too growing up, and I'm sure many adults will relate to this aspect of growth in their past. Carefully scrutinizing your child's friends is thus crucial, even though doing so is risky, as the child, if stubborn, would not listen. Sometimes, just knowing who these friends and the parents are is sufficient, and also bear in mind that the other parents are fighting with the same dilemma.

My son had lots of friends. Most of those I knew and was familiar with were those with whom he grew up in our social circle, but many of his post-high school friends were young people I knew little or nothing about. I wanted to know them more, but he didn't bring them home much, and never really introduced them to me in honesty. Their movements around were usually relatively suspicious but adolescent, and I tried to believe that it was cause for concern only in my head. I can't speak for his mother, but could tell that she too was in a juxtaposition, for every now and then, she'd complain to me about the character of his friends. One thing I hated most about some of his friends was those saggy pants they carried around, and then the dreadlocks on their hair. I also hated the smokes and those poorly-phrased speeches they called rap. I could not stand nor tolerate most of their lifestyle choices, but chose to remain reticent until he would reach a matured age and realize these follies himself. And of course I became scared of him and what could happen to him that could affect us all, if caution and reprimand wasn't activated. We must not let this happen to us for it gets increasingly disturbing when we do. We need to seek immediate help when we sense that something is wrong with our adult kids. Sometimes, if not all the time, they depend on us parents for redemption and will rarely do anything to jeopardize sanctity at home. I can't turn pages back now, but many of you can, and I trust that you would listen to this remark wisely. Junior was a very loving and caring young man, who needed a lot of direction, and I feel like I failed him because I took things for granted and cut him a lot of slack for so long. And now that I realize that I needed to intervene and monitor him and his every movement more acutely, time ran out on me. But I am sure he himself would want me to understand that it is okay to move on and stop lamenting on something that I can't change.

He would want me to tell every parent to institute greater involvement in the lives of their kids and be particularly more cautious when there are significant changes in their respective tendencies. Having detailed and informative discussions with our children can't be overstated as a very brilliant idea, but sometimes these details actually yield diminishing returns from our initial intentions, and end up derailing or misguiding the kids even more. This is particularly true on sentimental and sensitive issues that could poison the minds of kids and cause them to believe avoidable false and uncomfortable social malapropisms. I always tried as much as I could to avoid such discussions with my boys. But I couldn't tell whether or not some uncle, or aunt, or even their mother could have been mistakenly having talks with them on adult emotional issues, that could have blown off his mind, and then given room for depression and/or radical behavior—assuming that such could have been the foundation for Junior's explosive cantankerousness.

3.   The language, tone, and expressions we use at home definitely have a role to play in the lives of our children. Vulgarity absolutely should be avoided when our children are around us, and cursing them or other spouses should be forbidden. Once they realize that the home is becoming too unfriendly for them, they put on their obstinate gear and seek solace elsewhere, and sometimes the elsewhere brings them more nuances than what they may have been facing at home—but with a friendly atmosphere to depend on. We must never let our children to depend on outsiders for comfort lest they start enjoying the outside influence, which of course is always suited to accommodate foreign values inconsistent with those that we have in place for them. Teach them to agree to disagree in a respectful manner, and make sure that they understand the reasons or laws of curfew as a disciplinary measure and not mere parental punishment. It is absolutely important to get them to depend entirely on you for wisdom and provisions, so have honest discussions with them on your affordability and self-sufficiency without leaving the impression that they must be like you, if you are well to do, or unlike you if you're broke, is an important factor.

COPING WITH THE LOSS
OF A DEAR ONE

Feeling either rebuked, shellacked, or even deeply frustrated wasn't going to exonerate the guilt and painful feelings resulting from the tragedy of the sudden death on my son. To be able to move my family forward, I needed to have a clear conscience that would enable me move myself first, and then all in my family; but this state of mind was only going to be realized if we avoided the tempestuous feelings of the loss that had now settled into our minds. The Pandora's box, or whatever we choose to call this ordeal, was now open, and I needed to try to close it. How to cope with the tragedy varied in very many different ways, and for very many different reasons, and each attempt to dismiss a feeling of guilt or blame gave rise to another hypothesis. Assumptions that my boy, his mother, and I were on everyone's thoughts was obvious, but all those regular words of consolation and concern had stopped coming in. Some people were even bold enough to raise opinions that they had avoided when the death was still fresh. But the one person whose opinion mattered most was gone, and only he could answer my pending questions and bring me satisfactory peace of mind. Nonetheless, I had to come up with some vital coping mechanisms for me and for Taku, who still didn't like to express his feeling much on this sad and unfortunate incident.

We all had been silent for a while after the big holiday season, and I had put off writing for that period, to be able to try to enjoy all the celebrations. But that was practically difficult, for the absence of my social master, Junior, was conspicuously present wherever I went. And the questions about what happened to him didn't stop coming to me, making it even harder for me to cope with my grief. I took some time to reflect on this poem I had written a while ago, also pondering why I had written it. It was about Silence!

SILENCE

Silence is the answer that is forever dominant.
It is the ego that restores passion and indulgence;
And the heart that ruptures vulnerably.
Silence is the choice that flees regret-ability,
It is the drive that opens the mind, to see and
realize that
Hate and love, fall on opposite sides of the same
coin,
Which when flipped, projects the image of only
one side,
and that side alone.
Silence is the speech that expresses the shocks
and surprises
From the discomforts of life.
It is the message that accepts and eats reality,
And enables the silencer to sort out delusions.
Silence is the weapon that provides "pouvoir,"
To battle the unforeseen mistakes.
It is the victory that awaits proclamation; and
only then is
Silence silently destroyed.

Coping with these unforeseen circumstances can be circumvented, accelerated, and subjective in so many ways. Coping with loss or any tragic and regrettable situation is a relative mechanism, which depends a lot on individualistic representations. Any one individual may be able to cope better and/or differently from another individual, even when confronted with the same or similar circumstances. A parent or relative of a deceased may be able to accept the circumstance surrounding his or her ordeal, while some other parents and/or family members may continue to be in denial for an identical loss. Whether the coping is in denial or in acceptance, the ultimate goal and expected outcome remains the same. For the fact that something has happened does not depend on whether or not we accept or deny it. Rather, it depends on our strengths, for as individuals we seek to find rational and realistic ways to move on without exhaustive lamentations. It thus depends on our enthusiasms to use the ordeal as a learning experience, and to rectify our mistakes of the past to enhance a brighter and more productive future. Lamenting on uncontrollable situations could be perceived as an attempt to preserve the guilt of conscience, which, of course, could only lead to more pain from unexpected painful tragic contingencies.

Yen-Mary Njoka, resident in Chicago, Illinois, my elementary and high school sweetheart sister and friend, had lost her son a few years back in his sleep too and was still learning to cope with the pain of this loss. Note that there is no timetable for coping. Some days you could be so preoccupied with other things in your life and take a short break from the constant memories and reflections, but the feelings of sadness do resurface right back when you think you have a moment to relax from those day-to-day commitments. Mary celebrates all of her son's special days, expressing the glorious days she had with him while he lived. And whenever we communicate, she tells me how difficult it was, and still is, for her to cope with the fact that she is never going to be with him here on earth again. And who knows what the other life upstairs embodies? At first, my advice to her was always that she should remain strong, for God knows why it had to happen to her that way. I told her God loved him more, and now know that these were just blanket statements, without knowledgeable justifications. No one actually knows what happens when we die, and we can only believe and use the scriptures to find solace and peace to cope with these painful frustrations. Yen promised never to let go of her good memories with her dear son, and I now see why for I too have been holding tight to the memories of Junior—wondering why I was not been allowed to trade places with him instead.

Coping is sometimes just a postponement of grief. When you lose a loved one, you wake up each morning with thoughts of him or her on your mind, and then you go to bed every night with similar thoughts. You struggle with the understanding or lack thereof, of where in your vivid imagination he or she would be, and what he or she could be doing while there. So the question "how are you coping?" or the statement "I can't cope with this situation" would be mere expressions of our desires and frustrations and have little or no exactitude on our actual states of mind. What we need to remember to be guarding against during this difficult period is the control of our anger and bitterness. It is okay to be angry after such an ordeal of such magnitude befalls you, but holding onto the anger for a very long period can only do you more emotional and even physical harm. Letting go of these feelings may not be as easy as it may seem to be, but mindful of the fact that no amount of anger can reverse the situation, the prudent way to go about it is to cut your losses and move on to more productive pastures. Focus, therefore, on what you have left, and ensure that whatever you missed, to be able to prevent it from happening, should never be missed again. There are just no right or wrong feelings to demonstrate under these circumstances, and feeling low-spirited about such devastation will certainly be admonished differently by different people in each individual case.

Another coping methodology to emphasize is the seeking of support from different groups. These groups could be made up of family members, church brethren, schoolmates, or alumni groups, friends from all walks of life, and so on. Some people prefer to deal with their grief alone in their private ways, and this is perfectly normal; but sometimes, solitude adds depression to an already existing predicament and holds that individual down even longer than necessary, because of all the painful emotional reflections and setbacks. It is for this reason that I would recommend a group setting for people who wish to come out of the melancholy faster. Being a dynamic member of our community, I have been practicing both ways, and they seem to be working for my family and me. In a nutshell, our grieving process has appropriately allowed the elements of denial, anger, haggling with moods or mood swings, depression, and acceptance; and all these factors are enabling us to embrace the life that we have ahead of us and to move on to other things that we need to do to survive. There is no doubt that this process has been extremely difficult, and still is, but at some point, one has to come to terms with the finality of loss in preparation for when our own time will come.

Some Tips on How to Overcome the Loss of a Loved One:

1. Patience. Even in grief, we must be patient with ourselves. We must understand the particular circumstance under which our loved one left us and realize that it might have been unavoidable, and could have been for his or her good. Many examples could be cited, such as the unhealthy conditions that could have become a burden on him or her, affecting even on the entire family, and/or the mere fact that his or her time as God allowed was up.

2. It is definitely ambiguous to nurture unrealistic expectations about life. Only our maker knows with certainty what the future holds for everyone. So we must revise and adjust our expectations to accommodate all the realities of life and know that anyone of us can be called at any time. Whether it be accidental or through a protracted illness, it will come, and age won't be a determining factor, so we must live with such expectations.

3. I always charge myself to worry about the things that I can change and not those that I can't change. So when my boy went to be with the Lord, I immediately activated this personal philosophy and started dealing with the fact that I could never change the fact that he was gone. We must accept what we cannot change, even if it is the death of a child.

4. There is often a tendency to get stuck on uncontrollable situations as grief, sometimes because we want people to

appreciate our passions and loyalties; but I say it is more important to find strength in others, than try to impress them during such misfortunes. We are all humans and have a commonality in the way we perceive tragedy, without the need for invitations into compassions, which we already possess.

5. Time is always of the essence, and we have to recognize its infinity. Being infinite also means no one will live forever, and in as much as we want to go in the order in which we came, we are destined to go when our Big Father calls us. All we need to do is prepare ourselves to be called, so that we can go to the place that Christ has prepared for us when our bell rings. I had this on my mind before my son died, and still live with it even as I write.

6. The experience of loss of a dear one, though different this time around, is not new to me, particularly because I have lost so many siblings over the years. I am relatively beginning to create some value in this experience, knowing with certainty that there is a time to live and a time to die. With this in mind, I am trying to ready myself for my own death—a difficult thing to say because most people live as if they will never die. My friend Jimmy Njimbong hates to listen to me procrastinate on when I will die, and I can't remember how many times I have told him to enjoy and celebrate me whenever he can, for the call could come any day. And sometimes, such bluntness keeps him away from me for long periods of time.

7. Blaming oneself for unforeseen tragedies is a big mistake too. It is true and obvious that no one would allow such painful losses to happen, if we could tell when they would happen before they happen. So no need to blame yourself when such fate meets you. Just embrace it and count your blessings. Confront your emotions and release undue tensions. Nourish your soul in the process and affirm yourself positively, trying as much as you can to own your new reality. Feed yourself physically and spiritually well, and don't

forget to allow your total experience on your sad ordeal to serve as catalyst for productive change.

Junior's mother didn't seem to be finding it easy to cope with the loss of her son and was constantly in touch with my brother and me to express her grief. Taku had told me she was attending some counselling sessions in Fairfax. I knew how difficult it was on her and had told her to go easy on herself, for there was nothing she could do to reverse what had already happened. I wasn't interested in asking any questions about the past, knowing that that would just increase the chances of an unproductive blame game. This is what I told Gilbert when he said Grace wanted to know what decision he and I had taken on her suggestion for a memorial celebration:

Gil, I am certainly not oblivious to the fact that we all as Junior's parents, brother, uncles, and aunts feel guilty that we all failed him, or maybe that he failed us, depending on individual perspectives; but whether or not this predicament would have been averted is now an unattainable diabolical dream, conditioned to do nothing productive now that we all are struggling to move on with what we have left of life. There is no doubt on my mind that we all shall routinely wake up in the mornings with thoughts of Junior and go back to bed at night with similar thoughts. It is thus important to reiterate the need for us all to stop unfruitful lamentations on the fact that he is gone, mindful of the fact that we can never change the truth that he is no longer with us. He will continue to live in us every day though, an unchangeable fact too. We must not be impugned by this.

Anger exacerbates bitterness when we hold on to it for long, and this doesn't make the anger more affectionate because we have displayed painful emotions. I can say with precision that I have become quite experienced with emotional pain and the coping of the loss of a loved one, and you too are not far behind me since my loss is always your loss. I know the difference between a loss any loved one and the loss of a child. At the entrance of my house is my shrine of lost loved ones, and having to add my son to the picture frame has been one difficult exercise for me. I reflect every day on Joy, Victorine, Angeline, Irene, Mom, and Dad, and bringing Junior on board was absolutely devastating. I hold on to all of them this way, and they all live in me every day whenever I leave or come home. In your house too is Junior's poster and all your other pictured memories. In Grace's house is Junior's poster, which even his nephew adores and kisses. All these pictures need only reflections on the glorious times that we had with him when we had him with us.

I remember like it was just yesterday when Grace called me to report that Joy had died in an accident on the Victoria-Bamenda road in 1992. I remember just like yesterday Rose's call from Yaounde to report on Victorine's passing after surgery in Senegal in 1996. I remember like yesterday your calls to report on Angeline's and Irene's departures in 1998 and 2000, respectively. I remember Bro Ste's calls to report on the deaths of Mom and Dad in 2012 and 2015, respectively. And of course I remember my call to you and Taku's call to his mom on that fateful night of June 29, 2018, that has brought us to this page. I am not Job in the Bible, but can relate to what is written about him. Memorial manifestations are actually social inclusive events that do little or nothing to provide the desired closure that we seek, which is why I haven't bothered to memorialize your sisters and parents. I love to celebrate life, not death, but this in no way should minimize Grace's desire to memorialize and celebrate Junior. This is perfectly okay by me, and you too, and Taku says he's on standby for any decision taken. It's got to be a family affair though, including her siblings and close friends. That's what I think Junior would want, being the dynamite that he was in the community. He was a lover of life and people and told Taku and me on our last outing on Father's Day, three or so weeks before his death, he was trying to regain control of himself to make his whole family proud. I had just given them a short important talk on what to expect and do if something were to happen to me mindful of my cancer prognosis in 2003. Little did I know that my boy would go first. Funny!

As difficult as it is to make this unfortunate pronouncement, Junior had become relatively recalcitrant and cantankerously made quite a few miscalculations on his life choices. But none of us could foresee that the consequential outcome would be death, which in retrospect is the most devastating outcome that has come our way.

So death came to us, and we must accept our fate. Nothing we can do now to change this outcome. Holding onto emotional pain is counter-productive and can only cause unproductive spite and hate that divides loving people. On my part, I am trying with extreme difficulty to refrain from the retrospection of these painful reflections and recommend that all who love our boy should do same, especially his mom. The loss of a child is obviously the most difficult thing a parent should ever have to bear, and the emotional pain is equally excruciating though not in a physical way. And I know so because I am fighting to overcome such painful emotions too. I have however chosen to be strong for Taku and all of you, rather than give up and cause you all even more pain to have to deal with. And if the Lord were to call me home today, I would want you to make Taku, JJ. Evan, Victoria, and all the others understand that it is okay to go, for even the scriptures teach us that there is a time to live and a time to die.

Matthias Ndzi Waindim and I go a long way back to 1980 when we both lived and worked in Douala in the Cameroons. Meeting Matt in destitute at Dr. Ghangha's house upon my arrival to Minneapolis for his wife's funeral gave me chills, for I understood and felt what he was dealing with. I had "been there, done that." He had indicated to me when I buried Junior that he couldn't attend the funeral because his wife, Celestina Neng Waindim, was down with pancreatic cancer, suffering all kinds of associated complications of it. My plans with Chris to visit them in Minneapolis got postponed time and again for logistic reasons, and I was completely flabber-gasted when Matt finally mustered the courage to call and inform me about Tina's passing. He said he had been trying to spare me the pain since he knew what I was still going through from Junior's loss. Quite reasonable of him; and now he too is bound to join the mourners' club to start experiencing the pain of the loss of a dear one. Death has no isolation and can visit any home at any time. What a great loss to Matthias and his kids, and to her parents who were there present in Minneapolis, not forgetting her brother, Francis Fultang, who is also my friend. Members of our Kom community in the US came out to Minneapolis / St. Paul in numbers to bid Celestine farewell in a stylish and befitting coordination of events, and I have decided with Matthias to include his testimony in my book as a way of keeping a lasting memory of his final thoughts to his dear wife.

Matthias's Testimony to Celestine:

Tina, how sad it is to write of you in the past tense. Why so soon and at your prime? It hits me like an avalanche, and I don't even know where to start eulogizing your person. Still hallucinating that I have to be talking about you in "were, was" instead of "is, are"— expressions I will only come to terms with on my last breath. What a scary Saturday morning it was, when I thought you were sleeping with us, whereas you were gradually sleeping into the Kingdom of the Almighty. Hoping against hope, I was still waiting to hear differently from the doctors. It now dawns on the kids and me every second. The past two and half years have been a roller coaster to all the best hospitals and doctors you have been to and besides, and your faith in the Lord kept you going, but God has retired you home. Even in your most vulnerable moments, you still stood up for your family, friends, and community. What a model you were and still are. You touched so many people in different phases of life, and that indelible ink will be engraved in their minds forever.

We had our personal moments of excitement all these decades, and for the first time we had to spend Thanksgiving, Christmas, and New Year without running around the house to put a smile on everyone's face. Honie, I am just thinking how the rest of these festive days will be like—never the same, I guess! The thing that consoles the kids and me the most is no more sickness, no more pain, and I know you are looking down on those you have left behind, especially upon us—your family. We were blessed with wonderful children; Karen, Daryl, Chelsea, and Afuambom that you nurtured to be great and exemplary, and yet you have departed too soon to lead them into adulthood.

Tina—NaNabs, you were not only a loving and caring wife/mother; you were a wonderful person. You were friendly, kind, meticulous, and above all, family virtues were an embodiment of you. The love of God conquers all odds, and your church community where you worshipped is just speechless for having lost a benevolent Christian. We part in body, but not in soul, and there will come another day when we will not part anymore. Love you and will forever miss you! You are my Rock-star!

Love, Matthias Waindim

It is truly painful to lose a loved one, and the evidence of this notion is clearly visible each time we go to a funeral. This pain of loss is individualistic and permanent, and because of our lack of understanding of the concept of death, we will be left to imagine what happens to us when we die, and where do people really go when they die? Christ is the answer of such difficult questions, and it is prophesied that we should trust in the Lord, and He will give us rest!

CHAPTER SEVEN

COMMUNITY ROLE AND RESPONSIBILITY

When Mrs. Hillary R. Clinton wrote and titled her book, *It Takes a Village* (to raise a child)," the entire world got alarmed by this awareness of a fundamental principle of childbearing in society. But this proclamation wasn't new to me and many in our American-African communities, since we are fully conversant with a community-style pedagogy or a collective parenting style. The Secretary Clinton approach can be obtained by getting information directly from her book; but I am going to try to address the roles and responsibilities of the community in my setting to reflect why I think raising kids is also a community affair. Grace and I gave birth to Junior and Taku, but their growing up, just like the growing-ups of Lambert and Becky, Visisebom and Nambu, Raisa, Stephanie, and Vinielle, Papa T and Margaret, Melai, Sandra and Jesse, Emade, Amina, Marlene, JJ, Evan, and Victoria and many many more was a community affair that we all as parents felt comfortable with. Whether or not we were shunning our responsibilities is a subject for another book, but we all definitely had concerns for one another's child, and seemed to be collectively enjoying it.

Securing the progressive freedom of all our kids has been exceptionally important to me, and my friend Christmas Ebini and myself have had this discussion many times, over and over again. Even last night while I was sleeping, my phone beeped. It was Christmas sending me one of his poems. He enjoyed poetry, and I enjoyed it too. So this night I decided to immediately respond to his poem with a poem, which I composed with sleep in my eyes. We were meticulous about our passion for our kids, but never at any time did we limit such passion only to our biological kids. He was there for me when Junior died, and I was there for him when his daughter graduated from college; but even at such personal times, we still found time to discuss our Ambazonia struggle for the restoration of independence and self-determination, and what we wanted it to become with such realization. We understood all the difficulties of leadership and, more importantly, the difficulty of raising funds to fight against an already established country like LRC. But we always agreed that we couldn't give up the fight because so many of our Southern Cameroonian kids had already sacrificed their lives for the cause.

Restoration of independence was thus the only acceptable option, but getting unity from all southern Cameroonians was still a big problem. Everyone had his or her view, some productive and some unproductive, but all with the conviction that their perceptions were the best. Compromise was difficult to get, and sentiments were regularly egocentrically high. But I had only one worry in my head when I reviewed the reasons for the in-house fighting, asking the rhetoric question what about all the kids whose future we had destroyed with the great desire to achieve success, which, if unattained, would leave behind catastrophic results? Something needed to be done and fast, but how to bring everyone on the same page was the hard truth. I will share with you Christmas's poem, and then my poetic response, because we all believe in the role the community has to play in securing happiness for all our children and all our countrymen and women:

Patriotic Chant for heroes
Christmas Ebini

Patriots of our land
Great warriors of our revolution
Bearers of our armory

For peace and justice
The brave ones of ambaland
You have fallen in battle
Willingly paying the price
To free your land and people
With smiles on your faces
You conquered fear and cowardice
Unlocking the chains of slavery
Freeing your fatherland
The great and prosperous ambaland
All I wanted was to be there with you
To share in your patriotic glory
But destiny had a different thought
That I should bear testimony
Of your ultimate sacrifice and courage
And write this chant for you
So your people now and generations
Would never in their existence
Forget the match and fall
Of the great ones of our national pride
As we place your lifeless bodies below
Returning your souls to our ancestors
You become the fertilizer of prosperity
The shields that protect us in battle
The lubricant that fuels our armory
The silent voices that give us courage
To match on and lay possession
Of the freedom and independence
You paid the ultimate price for
Our brave heroes
You are the architects of our fate
Engrained in the walls of time
For your massive deeds and sacrifice
With your blood as ornaments of joy
And what may seem as idle show
Strengthens and supports our resolve

Leaving no yawning gaps between
Your bodies are the building blocks
For the structures that we must raise
For they are filled with materials
Truly shaped and fashioned for justice
For as builders wrought with care
You make us do our work as well
Our brave one, our heroes
You are beautiful, entire and clean
For the gods see from everywhere
As you stood on the hills of time
For such things remain unseen
As those who say behind you
May naivety be bound to despair
In the face of challenges and fear
Your sacrifice still sends hope
Exposing hidden camps of victory
Of bells of freedom with your blood.

Obviously, a good poetic expression about our struggle to restore our self-determination and independence, and with sleep in my eyes, I wrote:

POOR AMBA KIDS

Would you do us a favor and redirect the cause?
Would you do us a favor of redemption, and
*   revamp our delight;*
To struggle and conquer, but not struggle to
*   fail;*
Would you reach out to our sons, and daugh-
*   ters too,*
And comfort them some more before they falter,
*   from the stress of deaths?*
Am I mad or going mad, and seeing something
*   which we all should be seeing,*

Without the strength to fix it for me, for you,
and for all,
Brother, is it true that our courage is weaken-
ing, or why is our love
of country so different from the love of country
that we all know and want?
Would you summon every leader, and summon
me too;
To direct and redirect the shifting focus, to the
sanity of our kids?
We are not there yet; we can get there, but not
like this.
And now that we drown; would you call in
more paddles, before we sink?
I sleep in tears, and wake up with more tears;
and trust only in you now;
That you can make it happen, and stop my
children from all of these deaths,
So they can keep shooting, but only shooting
to kill, and to liberate us from all of this
mess.

Prince Kafain E. Mbeng Sr.

That weekend was jam-packed with lots of community events that I had invitations to attend. There was a traditional marriage ceremony for my dear niece Sandra Mubang to Fred Yonghabi, and I was compelled to be there. Sandra was my flower girl at my wedding in 1992—a year before Junior was born—and had now grown up to start her own family. All family and friends were there, and it was like a community affair. There was also the memorial service for my friend, David Achidi Sama, who had gone to meet his maker in 2006, shortly after he had called me to pick him up from his Gainesville, Virginia, home on one unfortunate fall night, when his world was falling apart. David was a good man with a good heart, and everyone in the community liked and adored him. My heart still bleeds that he is forever gone.

There was also an inauguration ceremony somewhere that Ali Sule wanted us to attend, but I managed to convince him that I could only be at one place at a time. So I made it early to church for the David service, and then settled in for the night at Sandra's ceremony, where my participation was highly in expectation. I decided on a no-show for a "rendezvous" with Christmas late that night at the Sama reception. And that is how we functioned in our community, everyone playing a role in everyone's life—maybe. It is exactly what I mean when I say in my claim that raising kids was a community affair in our circle of friends and relatives. Unlike in some foreign cultures, we adored living and carrying on together, even on our personal glories and misfortunes—which was exactly the case with the shock of Junior's passing. The community came together to participate in the funeral, and this made it bearable for my family and all its extensions.

The decision to tell this story is a way of appreciating our community of friends and family in all walks of life, and to increase awareness and readiness; for most of the time, we take eventualities for granted and forget that death does not give advance notice before the call is made. It may also be important to note that it is not everyone in the community or neighborhood that is on your side even in a difficult time like time of loss. One of my cousins had mistakenly knocked down a neighbor's sixty-dollar mailbox stand, and despite the circumstance, the neighbor was so upset that he chose not to wait but to confront my wife immediately for compensation. I sent my brother, his wife, and my wife with two hundred bucks to try to plead and settle, but in reluctance, they just handed the whole amount to the neighbor who was glad to receive it, I guess. Knowing my plight, I had expected the neighbor to be more supportive and sympathetic, especially since I had taken time to announce to every immediate neighbor that I was going to be having an influx of sympathizers on that day. Then shortly afterwards, my son, Taku, would get up one morning and find a note on his windshield attached to a bag of McDonald's trash that he was an "asshole" for littering. My boy was reasonably upset and taken aback with such insanity, and all I could do was comfort him and warn him to be careful when he got in and out of his car. Even if the trash had been his, which of course wasn't, calling him an "a-hole" was hateful for a stranger, and there was no way of knowing who this cowardly orator was, even though I had my suspicion. Most of my neighbors were good people though, and we all respected each other's privacy. There are all kinds of individuals in every community, and expecting the best from everyone is unpractical even when one is dealing with a personal loss.

I had just returned from visiting Junior's grave when Randy and Dan called to report that my sister had been admitted to the Bamenda General Hospital. While I was still struggling to subdue my emotions from the thoughts of Junior's absence and all the consequences, the prevalent killings of our Amba kids, and now Rose's health, Regina forwarded a speech of consolation and inspiration by Pope Francis that provided restitution to my anxiety. She too had Junior on her mind all the time, and I knew exactly how she felt from her constant expressions and reflections. I like to share this divine message for public consumption.

> *You can have flaws, be anxious, and even be angry, but do not forget that your life is the greatest enterprise in the world. Only you can stop it from going bust. Many appreciate you, and admire you and love you. Remember that to be happy is not to have a sky without a storm, a road without accidents, work without fatigue, relationships without disappointments. To be happy is to find strength in forgiveness, hope in battles, security in the stage of fear, love in discord. It is not only to celebrate the successes, but to learn lessons from the failures. It is not only to feel happy with the applause, but to be happy in anonymity. Being happy is not a fatality of destiny, but an achievement for those who can travel within themselves. To be happy is to stop*

feeling like a victim and become your destiny's author. It is to cross deserts, yet to be able to find an oasis in the depths of our soul. It is to thank God for every morning, for the miracle of life. Being happy is not being afraid of your own feelings. It's to be able to talk about you. It is having the courage to hear a "no." It is confidence in the face of criticism, even when unjustified. It is to kiss your children, pamper your parents, to live poetic moments with friends, even when they hurt us. To be happy is to let live the creature that lives in each of us, free, joyful and simple. It is to have maturity to be able to say: "I made mistakes." It is to have the courage to say "I am sorry." It is to have the sensitivity to say, "I need you." It is to have the ability to say "I love you." May your life become a garden of opportunities for happiness... That in spring may it be a lover of joy. In winter a lover of wisdom. And when you make a mistake, start all over again. For only then will you be in love with life. You will find that to be happy is not to have a perfect life. But use the tears to irrigate tolerance. Use your losses to train patience. Use your mistakes to sculptor serenity. Use pain to plaster pleasure. Use obstacles to open windows of intelligence. Never give up ...Never give up on people who love you. Never give up on happiness, for life is an incredible show. (Pope Francis)

This message from the Pope's speech was actually so inspiring that I immediately asked Regina to share it with her sisters and other family members. It had everything to say about wanting to be happy, which was always my son's motto, "Wanting everyone in the family to be happy." Most, if not all, communities seek the same goals for their children, even if they do so with abiding cultural differentia-tions. And sometimes, some individuals in the community miscon-strue their roles and generally try to misguide vulnerable members of their communities with unsolicited and irrational advice. Let me take a minute to outline some misconceptions on this topic:

1. Becoming Community Administrators: I know of so many people in communities who, for one reason or the other (usually those who believe they are socially and financially well to do), take command and dictate or cause their dependents to adhere to norms that give them personal satisfaction and aggrandizement. Their intentions always seem to be palatable, and their care obvious, but whether they are actually boosting their egos or fixing a problem is sometimes a cause for concern and should be looked into if or when they confront us in times of emotional starvation.

1. It is always mesmerizing to me to listen to gossip in the community about what went wrong in someone's house, even before the promulgators or prognosticators would get a chance to hear the real story. Expect such gossip when your child suddenly dies on you, even if the gossip is in whispers behind your back. In our community, gossip always becomes public when tragedy hits; then the sub-jects of the gossip call each other and say, "I told you so." And my response has always been that they should have done more than just gossiping, if they knew how to sal-vage what they thought was coming. In my case, I categor-ically refused to discuss anything about my ordeal with any inquisitors, knowing fully well that they would be coming to me to hear what I had to say, just in order to be knowl-edgeable enough when open discussions were made in the community about my follies.

2. There is no doubt that the majority of people who come to visit a mourning parent do so because they actually care. There was no doubt that I was surrounded by the love of family and friends; and there was no doubt that they all meant well in consoling my family and me. But there was

also no doubt that there had to be one, two, or three who in good faith sort compassionate information only to cast blame at a later date; and to that I was extremely cautious, even if the blame wasn't going to be directed at me.

3. There usually are the protectors and conciliators of interests, and they usually exhibit their roles by policing situations and checking out for any anomalies. Some even project figures and costs, and start discussions on who will do what and when; and of course this is all good, except that they sometimes overstep their bounds, and then begin to plan more for themselves and less for you, becoming very disappointed when you try to stop them. I didn't let this happen to me for obvious reasons, but enjoyed all the love, suggestions, and care that facilitated my grief without controversy.

4. Generally speaking, all in our community of family and friends do all these things in sympathy of what has just happened to a member of the community, and without such active concerns, the variance of emptiness may set in and bring in forces of unfriendliness to the community. So for this reason, the role and responsibility of the community cannot be overemphasized. It is also important to note that we live in a nation that is saturated with multiple cultural beliefs, yet progressive in every facet of our daily lives. As Americans, we must never act as if our choices are all culturally perfect, or maybe superior to the others, when we exercise our community-style values of enhancing our cooperation in times of sadness.

Living with the memories of a dead child gets upsetting and difficult by the day, even when one chooses to move on with the rest of his or her life. You get up some days and everything seems to have fallen apart, then you try as much as God can allow you to redirect focus on other things of vital importance, but what could be more important than your child's life? Of course, the other children you have should be more important, and should be able to provide you with the strength to foster the pain, but their pain too builds up and adds to your pain—all this in silence. I sometimes wanted my death to come right away, but the consequent devastation on my poor Taku was overriding my emotional drive and preventing me from any desire to go without a proper placement of him, that would give him the comfort and security to move on by himself. My general outlook gave me visible anger that caused close family and friends to label me with OCD (obsessive compulsive disorder) in our small gatherings. Some others made compliments, even calling me a role model. I did not believe I could be one, but enjoyed it anyway. As I was reflecting on my fate on this Sunday morning, my friend again sent me a sarcastic comment he wrote on comrade (M) on our Patriotic forum that read:

> "Milan also manipulates Sammy, Brad et al and took all the MTB money. He also took all the citizens levy. The Milan man is very tough. All the money donated to Morisc, AGC, SCYL, SOCADEF, and even the money from SONARA and CDC, Milan manipulated all those folks and took the money. It was because of Milan that Cameroun could not host the African cup because all the money to build infrastructures was given to Milan. The man even has a private jet, which Biya hires from time to time. I hear the Investigations Bureau is still investigating Milan's involvement in the crashes of the Indonesian and Ethiopian planes. Milan has decided to finally grant Southern Camerooons/Ambazonia full independence for some personal reasons."

> By Christmas Ebini.

So funny! I couldn't laugh without adding my comic relief.

> Great sarcasm on our friend and co-freedom fighter, Milan. Milan has also tied people's hands from reaching into their pockets and handbags to donate to help our children and affected strugglers on ground zero. Milan has entered every head with the super mystical powers he has and changed every cell of reason to carry his name and receive his orders. Milan, Milan, Milan; how great thou art! Milan again, and again, Yes, Milan! You've truly gained your fame, and I urge you to continue doing whatever you're doing; for it must be working, if that's all we must talk about. I think I know you Milan; and Sissiku too; and still remember our brilliant integration in Greenbelt with Christmas, Elvis, and all the rest. We all must focus only on how to become free; all these shenanigans can only hold us back; so we must thus ignore all our weaknesses, and focus only on our collective strengths: and Yes Milan; you must not stop; for every contribution counts, and yours too. We are a people, and a prospective great people; and our enemy has become so intimidated by the fear of us, because they know we have been right all along, and rightly so. The Prince.

Then I came down to my office to open mail from the Fairfax Memorial Funeral Home that Taku had brought home the night before. The cause of death had been adjusted by the medical examiner to reflect accidental drug overdose. I had never heard of the drug fentanyl before this crisis and had no idea whether or not any vital organs were harvested from my boy's remains without my consent. But this wasn't of any real significance to me now or ever, as my wish was just to continue visitations in acceptance of a fate bestowed on me by the Good Lord. I had been planning to call Martin Wuno and his lovely wife, Emma, to compare notes, but the weekends were always busy with one thing or the other in our community, which had become more compelling than actually residing in the Cameroons where we all hailed from. Everyone in the community has a responsible role to play in the upbringing of all the lovely children we bear, and tragedy like mine and Wuno's and all others never held anyone back.

CHAPTER EIGHT

FINANCIAL RESOURSES CONCERNS

Very few people in our community in particular, and the world at large, usually ever seriously think about making allocations for the funeral costs of their children—reason, realistically, being that we never expect our children to die before us. It is a general consensus to purchase or secure life insurance policies in the event that if something were suddenly to happened to us parents, our children should not be left to suffer with expensive funeral costs. We hardly ever envision anything happening to our kids first. Which is why my existing life insurance policy didn't cover my son's funeral expenses. Nonetheless, he was going to be buried, and we were definitely going to bear the costs if that was going to happen. The first thing BJ said to me when he arrived town was that I should think about cremation for it was cheaper. But cremation was not a consideration I was ever going to be willing to make, not just for the cultural and traditional discrepancy, but for the fact that I am one who believes that we work hard and save funds against such rainy days, and that was certainly my own rainy day.

While his remains were still at the medical examiner's office, I summoned a meeting with his mother and sisters at the Fairfax Memorial Park Funeral Home. Taku and I were there on time, waiting, when everyone involved arrived. That is one meeting no one should cherish having. Emotions were visibly high, and sentiments were expressive enough for the sadness of days to come. The director was extending the usual courtesy of offering water and more time if we needed to calm or cool down. After doing this many times before, it was certain she knew what to expect and do, and she kept switching just the right buttons as we struggled to agree on the options that she was presenting. She immediately could read that my main problem was not how to pay for the services, but how to give Junior a befitting burial. She took time to walk us through the process, explaining everything about every cost. Then she took us in to an inner section where caskets were kept, and I left the very difficult task of selecting the coffin and its accessories to the honor of Taku and his mother. The vault too. Some of the suggestions were actually not necessary, but I decided to get them, just to get everything right, and be done with it satisfactorily without having to make another trip in there.

Fairfax Memorial Park has its uniqueness for having everything in one location. There was the funeral home, the chapel, and the cemetery, which meant that I could have everything done without having to move my son around much. Even the reception hall was about a mile and a half away. They would collect the remains from the examiner's office and let me know when they had him so I could plan a private family visit alone with him, even before he was prepared for the funeral. My uncle Dr. Chiabi and his wife would tell you how difficult this day was on us. Actually, Aunty Emma could not even go in to see Junior, and Grace will remember this day as the worst day of her life for the rest of her life. Just so that you know, there is a variation in funeral costs depending on where one chooses to have one. There were so many reasons why I chose Fairfax, not only as a citizen of Fairfax, but because it was close to our home, and we would be able to visit often. My friend Victor Njabu Njomo was buried there too, and he was very fond of Junior when they both lived. Mildred Ayeah, my nephew Tony's wife, was buried there too, making that park to become a regular spot for our family and friends to pay memorial visits and bring flowers.

My new normal life would now be punctuated by multiple family- and community-orientated concerns, and March 22, 2019, became no different when I left my house at dawn and drove down 395 going to work in DC. Reflections of my conversation with IG

Song, the KOM-USA president, about my opinion on a royal visit in June were still fresh on my mind, especially after receiving information that the Fon had difficulty returning to the palace because of the revolutionary battle in Baingo. His people were dying at war, which must be why I told IG that the timing would be inappropriate. Still pondering on this as I drove on, my phone beeped continuously for a good portion of my trip, causing me to pull off at a -Eleven on Washington Boulevard, to ensure that my attention wasn't badly needed somewhere.

First two messages were from my friend and Chairman of RC of FRA, Elvis Kometa, wanting to inform me that he had been admitted overnight for diarrhea infection from eating bitter leaf soup. Then there was an emotional health update from my family's sister, Princess Nabs, an update which I must publish since Junior's passing had now placed me in the business of sharing precautionary experiences with my readers.

NABI'S Message: "Hi Ka, we've been quiet...I've not been doing well though. From swollen kidney to blood clot in the liver to fluid retention in the pancreas. The fluid in the pancreas was drained on Tuesday, and next week the kidney stone that has been lodged in my bladder since November—causing the swelling in the kidney— will be removed. That's my story and there you have it."

I had just rushed with Gilbert and Brown a few months back to visit her at the Johns Hopkins Hospital in Baltimore after her pancreatic cancer surgery, so this message literally brought tears to my eyes as I pondered about how much time she had. But she was a strong and determined woman and had told me that she would fight it all the way with all the might that she had left in her.

My reply to her text was: "Princess Nabs, So so sorry dear! Been thinking of you and particularly your plight, wishing and praying that it should painlessly go away. But all is in God's hands, and He alone knows best why He gives us what He gives us. Despite all in our early years, you are like a sister to me, and after taking all my sisters away from me, I plead that God should give me time with you, Nabi and Malai, and all the others who are also not doing very well right now; so Lord, please wipe my tears and give them the strength and health, to keep cheering me up, for I need them now more than ever. Or send me a message to give them, so they can have some understanding of your omnipotence! Nabi, I love you and will try to come visit with you this coming weekend. Hold onto God and He shall give you rest! Prince Kafain."

Even if I had made her distressed, I know it was ok, especially since she wrote back that, "This is the best prayer message I have ever received. Be sure that it left your mouth and heart straight to His ears. This has really touched my heart. Thank you so very much. You know there has always been a special spot in my heart for you. God bless you too and see you this weekend."

And of course Fien and I were there the following day, and we all had a long pleasant visit chatting and drinking. During this time, I also checked on Chairman Elvis Kometa's condition, and he reported well and out of the woods.

Back to my narrative on Funeral Cost Analysis: In consultation with Grace and her family and Taku, I decided to go ahead with funeral arrangements two weeks into the date Junior died. I hated to have to keep him for long in a funeral home and thought a quick funeral would also kick off an acceptance and closure process for all family members that would have serious concerns and remain terribly affected. When sudden death strikes, and because of the financial unpreparedness, some people in our community usually would call family meetings to discuss how to cover funeral expenses, and that would be quite a reasonable choice to make; but I decided on my credit-worthiness and personal contingency funds in order to avoid inconveniences and unnecessary expectations from family and friends. The only other obligator here was his mother, and whatever she would come up with was going to be perfectly sufficient to subsidize or offset the chunk of the projected costs. I also had the belief and strong conviction that people who were sympathetic would get through to me even without me asking, and of course they did, just as I too always did, and every little bit added up to augment what I had in my plate. Needless to name names, for they all know who they are, from KEY to Mr. P, and I am very thankful and appreciative of their help with all my heart. In our community, one is indebted to the people who are indebted to him/her because of the frequency of these deaths—an element of cooperation that provides supplemental funds during times of need, particularly in times of the passing of loved ones.

Back in my hometown of Belo-Boyo in the Northern zone of the Southern Cameroons/Ambazonia, records of all contributions in all socio-cultural events, including even funerals, were usually kept, in the event that it would be easy to determine whether or not someone was financially active in participation in the community. We of the SC/Ambazonian heritage in the States had definitely imported such traditions here, and I always made sure my name was on that list. I was therefore certain that the community would come through for me at this dire time, and of course they did, and in numbers too—an appreciable cost alleviation to say the least. We can rightly assert that this culture serves as a dependable informal life insurance policy, for so many of us have come to benefit and enjoy the augmentation to our meagre emergency funds and the likes of it.

The basic cost, embalming cost, casket and vault cost, visitation cost, in or out service cost, dressing cost, etc., at the Fairfax Memorial Funeral Home came to a total of $15,428.90. The gravesite cost, grave marker cost, burial cost amounted to $8,775.00. The hall for the after-burial reception costed $4,000.00, and all the decorations, food and drinks, etc., would be undetermined for obvious reasons. These costs need not scare anyone, for there are always other options, like cremation at up to $8,000.00, depending on individual funeral homes and packages. While I put down these costs, I must add that the thought of having to do this is not a very comfortable process in the minds of any struggling parent; but when it happens to you, you must do what you have to do to give your kid a deserving farewell. Grace, Taku, and all close family expected nothing less even if they didn't say so; and I was known for always notoriously wanting to do things on the high end, and this special occasion wasn't going to be any different.

A visit to check on Taku and me by Dr. Comfort Bonu, who had flown in from New Mexico to be with Grace for a few days, raised the emotions of the pain of Junior's loss again; but we all agreed that such pain was never going to go away. What we needed to do was to memorialize the goodness of his life and enjoy those memories, Comfort said, and after giving Taku some school allowance, she left and promised to return to spend more time with the whole family when we all will try to find ways to deal with our benevolent spirits or what was left of them. She said she understood how costly funerals were in this country and was so happy to know that we had handled our case without the kind of stress that was common about and, of course, quickly noticed my reluctance to want to have her worry about any supplementation. That was the kind of relationship we had cultivated over the years, even if we had stayed for years without remaining in touch as we needed to. She was a kind, caring, and concerned sister during my brief stay in Victoria in 1993—the year Junior was born—when she headed the preventive medical offices of that division, and I used to spend quite a lot of time in her office reading magazines for emotional distractions from some personal problems I had. She and Grace were really very close.

CHAPTER NINE

LESSONS LEARNED FROM THE LOSS

When the tragedy of death happens the way it happened to me/us, nothing in the world ever seems normal again. The guilt of having not done something to prevent it from happening becomes a daily pragmatic reflection, and the will to move on constantly gets impeded every time one thinks of his or her loved one. I have been struggling to overcome these feelings everyday now and wish to debunk the theory that such feelings usually go away permanently with time. They never go away, and if they do, they do so only when you too die. Seeking understanding and searching for solutions kicks in, but it is usually too late to find solace from answers that won't bring your loved one back. However, just knowing what actually happened is enough to comfort you and put you in a position to be able to console and advise others, also providing you the kind of strength required when in confrontation with the curiosity of members of the community in which you live. The first lesson you learn is how strong you are or may be in handling your emotions and the emotional pain of all people in your family.

One of the most important lessons to learn and teach about the loss of a child is the recognition of any existential problems that the child was facing in life. Most children do not manifest in the same way to similar problems and provocations, and it is always standard pragmatism to quickly identify any problems which our children are facing, before these problems become too difficult to control. I was certainly, but mistakenly, under the impression that my son was doing just fine. In spite of his misconceptions on certain personal choices he used to make, the thought of how such malapropisms would affect and alter his live was the last thing I centered my attention on, and now have learned that I was wrong, or at least not attentive enough. Not staying focused on the ball of discipline somehow left me with only a superficial view of the negative choices, and a strong belief that he was going to outgrow his recalcitrance and eventually realize the benefits of productive behavior. Not really knowing what my boy was dealing with, I am now bound to regret why I didn't take more redemptive action to rescue him even from himself, but how to have been able to do so is the billion-dollar question, and the learning experience that leaves me forever broken and unable to make wrong right. And I will just say, it is better to be safe than sorry!

As the first anniversary of Junior's passing closed in on us, his mother was becoming increasingly paranoid about the fact that he no longer was around with us, and her anxiety was resuscitated into a desire to do something exceptional that she believed would significantly quell her frustrations. I, myself, began to develop mood swings when anyone in the family requested any favors from me, particularly those that needed to be empathizing along with me for this great loss. The idea that they could have forgotten the stress that I was compelled to bear was getting to me, and brother Richard quickly identified and changed the tones of the dependencies to give me a much-appreciated break.

Juxtaposing on all upcoming travels to attend any social and cultural events on one hand, and the guilt of abandoning the memoriam of my son that was coming up constantly surfaced on my mind as I told this bothersome story—a load of emotions that I was now bound to carry everywhere I went and in everything I did. Staying calm and focused was still going to be the appropriate thing for me to do, a lesson I learned and followed the hard way. Assuming that everything was okay with everyone at home, when the contrary could be the case was a precautionary lesson to take special note of. It is always prudent to ensure the well-being of everyone in the family, even when you are home in your respective rooms. This is also true when the conviction is that someone is just resting. In our sleep, anything can happen, and sometimes, there is no distress call or cause for concern. We are therefore obliged to be one another's keeper in every sense of this phrase. Avoid locking the doors all the time for unnecessary privacy, or at least declare your nap lengths just in case.

I am my father's son: On fiduciary issues, Dad taught me never to be completely dependent on anyone to crack my nuts for me, for he said, "You enjoy them better when you crack them yourself."

Growing up with such a philosophy in mind has provided and secured me with confidence, and on many occasions, I have been able to handle some real difficult undertakings without the desperation for assistance as could have been expected otherwise. I have thus learned to live within my means—a visible realization conjectured during the planning of my boy's funeral. I was also able to learn at this time that while people empathize with one's misfortunes, they are only able to do what they can comfortably do, so expecting more from people would be unfair, unjust, and unproductive.

I have always been principled with my life choices and, as a result, have always categorically refused to be compromised on issues contrary to my beliefs. This discipline must be what hindered me from being more understanding of my son's delinquencies, and I am just now learning that maybe I should have cut him more slack than I did, even if that was going to cause me to deviate from my fundamental pedagogic philosophy. My adolescent years were not too different from his; my late old man would have testified (like father like son), but times and means were now different in totality. Growing up in a mission compound didn't stop me from jerking around with my friends all over Bafreng, and Joel, Edward, Stephen, Alfred, and Fabian would tell you that we tried a lot of boys and girls stuff and experimented on booze and smokes on some opportune occasions. Fortunately, we always knew exactly when to stop. We matured into self-making youngsters and took upon ourselves to seek progressive ventures like business and schooling abroad after leaving high schools. That is how I ended up in Nigeria and then later the States. We took up all kinds of odd jobs to support our independence and survived and built what we then had to start our own families and have our own kids. Most of my classmates have such similar stories to tell about how we each learned from our experiences. In the course of my adult life, I have learned so many life lessons, but none has been equal to the lessons I am now learning from the loss of my child. I have learned foremost that when you are home with your children and there is silence in the house for long, go around the house and check on every one of them. This is so true even for the adult kids. You are definitely never going to be yourself again when you wake up one day and one of your children is gone. The tragic memory will haunt you each time you go past their room, their school, and their everything; and the fact that you had no control over their destiny is a hard lesson to bear. We thus should spend each minute with our kids as if it was the last minute, for there is no telling when they can suddenly be taken away from us.

People in your circle of friends and family are usually there for you when they too derive some kind of pleasure from the closeness; and when such bond is by any means interfered with, a safe distance, is often created. I have learned this the hard way, but with appreciation. I had people that I thought were my confidants, and in every way possible; but they proved me wrong, and betrayed my trust, especially on matters relating to my matrimonial benevolence. So all that I may have said in confidence may probably have been misrepresented in my absence, and I could tell so by experience and observation. I'm sure I'm right to ascertain so in the events leading up to the troubles and passing of my son. But I'm not accusatory though, and not in justification of my follies and my failures, as all the faults must be absorbed by me and me alone. Life is one learning experience even under very contemptuous circumstances, and this particular experience, which keeps fluctuating, has become my Bible of life in my days and years ahead.

Now I don't leave home when I think I am in a bad mood, and so shouldn't you, and I ask myself every day what outcome would have resulted had I left home that day without checking on the sanity of my house. We'll never know! Not knowing that anything was abnormal in my house on that Friday, I could have decided to go hang out with Victor as I usually did. Taku and Del could have gone to sleep, not realizing the apathy, since it was in Junior's culture to sleep all day and then sneak out at night when he wanted to hang out with his friends. But God loved us so much to let things happen that way, and I am so glad the discovery was made by me, and not by Taku, for the trauma and shock would have a longer lasting effect on him than on me. This could turn his emotions upside down whenever he pondered or reflected on how his brother left him. It was rightly my duty as a father to ensure wellness in my house at all times, and I was doing just that even though I couldn't save my boy from untimely death, and have come to accept that it was all by the Will of God.

Asking questions about that day, and the days before and after, is not really to seek answers, for no answers will be satisfactory, and no answers will change any facts nor bring our boy back; but asking to know is a learning and teaching exercise that should provide clues to others in event they too should encounter such unkind eventualities.

Another interesting question hovering in my head that gives me chills is whether we in our attempt to resuscitate him followed proper CPR procedure. That was definitely my first real-life CPR experience, even though I had witnessed many before. It was Taku's too and, obviously, Delphine's first, despite her little training in nursing. And of course, performing such a technique on your son or brother must be absolutely unpleasant. I still have nightmares about it and can't stop imagining the drastic effects of it on Taku, whose bravery I continue to commend to this day. I think about the instructions from the 911 operator and wonder how she would be expected to know how someone is responding to lifesaving instructions on the phone; but again, that has to be the best they got, within the timeframe that they usually have. Take it or leave it! It is standard procedure, and they have saved so many lives with it, and it must continue to be that last hope, when we are faced with these emergency situations. Hypothetical thoughts will certainly clog your head, but all you have to do is to try to learn from any potential questions, that would serve no purpose other than make you feel that you could have done more than you were able to do. I had vehemently tried to change the outcome, but that wasn't what God wanted.

One year without my Junior had gone by real fast, but the closure of loss was far from over, as I and everyone else continued to show intense reflections of grief and regret that he was no longer with us. I organized a special family memorial service at the graveside, hoping to stay positive and put all agonizing sentiments behind; but it was noticeably clear that such sentiments never go away, and new ones even develop—such as the ones which my friend Jimbo tried to revive when he revisited the guilt and failures in executing appropriate responsibilities by everyone. Many who should have come didn't come, but even their conspicuous absence didn't affect how I felt on that day, for my main concern was to ensure that that day's focus was Junior, and indeed it stayed that way till the expressions and speeches that followed at home in the evening. My high school literature teacher, Mr. Sammy Arrey-Mbi, whose daughter too had just passed away a few months after my son, had told me to be prepared to ignore public opinion about how to deal with my pain, saying that such pain never went away, even with time as people generally suggest. This chapter of my life was therefore going to be with me forever, and all I had to do was to enjoy every unchangeable outcome of it.

A MOTHER'S PERSPECTIVE AND THE WOMEN IN HIS LIFE

Our last attempt to understand and address our son's plight would be when the three of us were in his Potomac hospital room on that last Monday morning; he would suddenly die four days later. While he was in bed, apparently sleeping, his mother and I tried to figure out what he was going through, or what could have gone wrong with his mental reflexes. An attempt by his mother to brief and update me on the history of how we had arrived at that point was overshadowed by our son's delusional outburst and chanting. He literally ordered us out of his hospital room, alleging that he knew our intention there was to discuss his choices and actions. His sudden reaction towards us was unbelievably frightening, and only then did I (we) immediately realize that something could be deeply wrong with him. Despite that, death was never in anticipation on any of our minds, and I can bet that even he did not think he would be dead by the end of the week.

A mother gets up one day only to realize that everything she feared could happen to her has actually happened. Then she opens her eyes wide open, and feels adrenaline rushing through her veins. She goes searching for answers everywhere, banging all doors all over, looking under all beds, and screaming at the top of her voice; then she realizes that her child is not responding to her calls because he will never be able to respond again. That is when she captures the true meaning of death, as hallucinations start vibrating in her head. She shouts out his name, and screams some more, and then realizes that she is not the only one shouting and screaming. Her kids are all screaming too, and their father is speechless in defeat, and all the people around her are furiously startled in confusion. Her brothers, sisters, and friends all marvel in the face of all these troubles. She wants to curse God and hate Him too, but she knows it was He who gave him to her in the first place. Her eyes wander into the skies to see if the scriptures are practically inscribed there somewhere, but the memories of her loss are so dire and daring that she chuckles and coddles as her pain deepens.

It is a new day, and the result is the same, and will always be the same every day now for the duration of her life. It then begins to settle in on her mind that it is all over, and she will never see or be with her child again, for he is forever gone. Tears and grief will not bring him back; anger cannot bring him back; and all the love she had for him will not bring him back either. Emptiness pounds and pounds, again and again at the door of her heart; her head aches, her blood pressure builds up really fast, and her voice cracks and fades into her head. All she thinks she has left is she, but the truth is that she has God left with her too.

Then the next day, she makes her next trip to the grave one more time, and many more times. She brings him an assortment of fresh flowers, to add to those left there by his father before she came, but this is all vanity now, and that is all she can now do to get some solace. "What is life?" she asks in rhetoric. "What a waste, and why me," she continues to ponder and soliloquize.

The loss of a child ranks very high or is at the top of the chart of the unpleasant things that a parent can bear, particularly a mother. There was no doubt at any time on my mind that Junior's mom would find it extremely hard to cope with his death. It is now evidently clear that that is the case, and I am going to try to categorize some motherly perspectives that may or may not be interesting to note.

Grace was Junior's biological mother and knew his psyche more than anyone else on earth. They were very close, and he confided in her a lot. This is not to say that he didn't confide in me, but his understanding of my code of discipline in my household made him believe that I would object, or try to be overly objective, or even scrutinize and prevent him from the simple things that he could easily get away with, if he dealt exclusively with his mother. Of course, this was a normal and common phenomenon prevalent with all children in our community. Mothers would most often vouch for their kids, and probably keep their secrets when they (mothers) thought they (kids) could get into some kind of trouble. Whenever Junior's mother envisaged big trouble, she would call that to my attention, though in a deflective manner, which was probably why I would sometimes decide to remain reticent on some of his disciplinary discrepancies. It was a culture practiced by most families, and there was a consensus in the community that it was a way to hold the family together.

I am quite sure that Grace would want to do things differently now, after such a devastating outcome, and I say so with no prejudice, as I myself would want to have another opportunity to make things right for my boy. She and I have come to learn a very difficult lesson, in the most ruthless fashion; but life must go on. We cannot change what has happened, and seeking pity or sympathy would be absurd. I continue to pity her though and wish her every ounce of redemption in her mourning process. I have thus chosen not to speculate on her state of mind as I pen down this memoir, for discussing her feelings of grief with her might be opening up old wounds for lamentations—a sentimental mistake if an analysis of root causes resurfaced. Her twin sister, Regina, has been there for her, and I know so because we spent some time together after the fact. She too needs emotional healing as a mother to Junior, and has been showing signs of her strength, when she and I exchange correspondences every now and then. Regina seems to be the adult in the room in spite of her own personal shortcomings. Once in every while, I endeavor to reach out to her, even if it is just to cheer her up, and I feel the same way as with her sister, about the mincing of sentimental expressions on our loss. It is different when I chat with Junior's male uncles though.

Their baby sister, Georgette, used to be my best friend and favorite after Judy, but I have not heard a word from her since. Maybe she is just busy, or maybe something is pissing her off. I know for sure that she too was quite broken-hearted, after that first terrible day, and throughout the funeral planning process; but I cannot nail the cause for the cut-off and silence, and sometimes it is prudent to just "let sleeping dogs lie," for lack of a better expression. Dominic, her husband, and I are in occasional communication, and he would have told me if there was any particular cause for concern.

The loss of a child is definitely one of the most difficult experiences a parent can bear, not only because of the death of the child itself, but because of the number of lifestyle compromises and adjustments that one is compelled to make to accommodate the ordeal. Intimate family relationships can collapse, if precautionary measures are not quickly identified. and at the same time, some bad relationships could also be re-energized. My honest wish has just been for all in Junior's extended family to continue to get along, as he would have wanted. That was one thing he always cared and worried about— people sticking together.

It will be social injustice not to bring in his sister, Liengu Anembom, who made him an uncle before his death. He, I am told, had a unique relationship with the baby, and his passing was very hard on the poor kid, even if he does not understand the meaning of death. Liengu and Junior had been siblings four-plus years before Taku was born, and the three of them had spent all their years together in Manassas and Woodbridge, with only a few punctuations.

Then there was Delphine. She and Junior, as I said in my opening rant, were just beginning to know each other's family sentiments. His visits home were not as often as should have been, and even when he did, he would sleep a lot during regular visitation hours. Delphine tried to influence my stance on strict discipline on his behalf, but my values and convictions were uncompromising. "Is Delphine home?" he would ask me sometimes when he called me and would make smart remarks when I tried to advise that he be respectful and add aunt to her name. But he did so in his usual teasing way, making sure that he was not misconstrued. They enjoyed cocktails together, and both thought I was unaware of it, but I was just happy that they were getting along well. He surely was enjoying his time at home, and rightfully so, and was actually planning to return to his room permanently. Taku and I were actually searching for a new bed for him on the internet on that afternoon, not knowing that the evening was going to alter our lives the way things unfolded. I wish I had checked on him in his room then, and to this day, that fact bothers me a lot. Even Delphine must probably be lamenting on the fact that she did not indulge him in the kitchen on that day as she usually did. His time had come, and I am sure nothing could have stopped him from going the way he did, I must conclude.

Just about two weeks before that fateful day, he had questioned me about his grandfather's funeral, which he missed going with me to attend. He strangely asked me if there had been any special Baptist or government honors given to Grandpa, and I showed him some of the pictures and videos on my computer that Uncle Chris had just sent. His question also reminded me of a statement the Baptist Education Secretary made to Honorable Paulinus Jua, and then to my uncle, Prof. Chia and me, that he, the secretary, had no records in his office of my dad—the very man who was one of the founding fathers of the Education Authority of the Cameroon Baptist Mission. My son did not like the sound of that story and thought it was so unfair for the secretary to disrespect his grandfather that way. During their short stay with grandpa in Belo, Grandpa had told them all he could remember about how the Baptist Mission had bought him over from the government to come and run their schools, and how he and Chief Ikome had become the first two supervisors of Baptist schools, after the American missionaries handed over the schools to the indigenes. Junior then declared that he was never going to let anyone belittle my services to any institution when I died, but little did we know that he would die before me.

Junior had a good perspective on some religious concepts and never missed an opportunity to want to lecture Taku and me, and sometimes his mother, on what he thought was happening in the religious world. A typical example of this was when he said, "People always rush to do evil and inappropriate things during the week, and then rush to church on Sundays, to confess and seek forgiveness, and then return and start doing the same thing over and over again from Mondays to Saturdays. I wish we could just do it right the first time, and stop pretending," he would conclude in his hyperbole of religious demagoguery. That was how he ended up easing the impact of the Baptist secretary's statement on my mind by trying to be funny or comic.

Petra and Elsie were my boys' godmothers and were always present in their lives. Elsie was probably the last woman in his life to have a conversation with him. Junior and her biological kids, Lambert and Becky, were always together and enjoyed spending their time with her. Petra adored them and provided for them and sent them lots of food each time I visited her with or without them. It was in her house that they were so thrilled to receive Bishop George Nkuo's blessing many years back. Then there was Laura, who says she mentored him in her own way. He used to say she had increased the number of Mbeng names in the family, a remark that only Junior would care to make. The women in Junior's life all cared about his well-being and would have done anything to keep him around much longer. And of course there were many more women in Junior's life, like his girlfriends, who shall remain nameless since he never really mentioned their names to me, neither did Taku. Pauline was quite fond of Junior too, and she and Victor had embraced my children just as I embraced theirs. We were like family, and I was very happy to bury Junior next to Uncle Njabu. Our trips to the Memorial Park have become relatively inclusive, and Pauline can attest to. Junior literally spent his last year with Pauline, and I told him it was okay, even though I insisted that he hang out there with Papa T as a visitor, and not a permanent guest. This was one of the issues his mother and I were trying to resolve, without knowing that our desire to amend some of this life choices would be stopped in such a forensic manner.

On one August Sunday morning, while on the phone with my brother and a therapist that he was introducing to me, my doorbell rang and his daughter, Kuoh Foinbu, came in from Kansas. Kuoh had visited with us for some time in the nineties before returning to Atlanta and Alabama and had been present at the funeral with the rest of her brothers and sisters. A year had already gone by, and she said she wanted to visit Junior's grave and check on Taku and me.

She is a special niece to me and a special daughter to my brother and has had her own share of emotional setbacks in her life that keep her on her toes all the time. Junior's passing had a striking effect on her—causing her to want to form a family group of their generation that would arrest unforeseen contingencies before they occur. Which I believe is how the Chiabi Family Reunion of November 2018 in Atlanta got started.

Aunt Nain and Uncle Kakwah lived in Michigan in 1993, and that is how Junior ended up being born there on September 7. Nain and Kakwah had now moved to Atlanta and would always call us to come down from Alexandria, Virginia, to Atlanta, Georgia, whenever they had an event at their residence. Many at times, Junior even insisted that we just drive down there to visit, so that Aunty Nain could drive him, Visi, and Taku to church, and then a hamburger and fries place on their way home. Both Nain and Ka were very much in his life, particularly because Ka and Grace were very close. After Junior was born, Kakwah and Nain were the ones who brought Grace and him to Alexandria, to leave them with Rose and Gerry, since I was still on my extended stay in the Cameroons. The Bretons and the Mbengs used to spend a lot of time together before Gerry's rise to their diplomatic missions abroad. Rose and Gerry had just returned home, and Grace was taking them to the grave, coincidentally on a day that Roy and I were out there visiting. So we all shared sentiments and emotions at the grave, and then retired for lunch at a Hilton restaurant nearby. Rose had had full powers over Junior as one of his mothers, and he, Junior told me he was naming Aunty Rose "Aunty Rose Two" in order not to confuse her with Rose, my sister, whom he referred to as "Aunty Rose One" since she was older. The news about Junior had absolutely devastated both Roses, especially my sister, causing her to refuse to talk to anyone for days, including even me. After eventually gathering the courage to take my call, all she said was, "We go do how nor," leaving herself complacent to any outcome.

Grandmas Mary Mbeng, Eugenia Shanklin, and Janet Davidson all had fun and high hopes for my boy, and especially so because of his exuberant personality. He was a fun kid that was always smiling, and they each had their personal reasons for his admiration, all of this without any of them actually spending any lengthy consistent times with him. Eugenia obviously saw him more often than Mary and Janet, because we visited her Princeton mansion every now and then. She gave him swimming lessons, carried him on her back the African style, and likened his looks to those of his grandfather in his youthful days. Out of these three grandmas, Janet was the only one with the unfortunate privilege to be present at his funeral, and my guess would be that Mary and Eugenia must have led the angels that waited for him at the gates of heaven.

Grandma Amina, Junior's maternal grandmother, is definitely still too confused about his death. In January of 1994 in Victoria, she and I had stayed up until the dawn hours on that day that I came in from Bamenda to see my baby boy for the first time. He was a four-month-old bundle of joy, and we both tried to protect and nurture him amidst all the mixed emotions of love. Amina is thus the only grandma who spent a lot of time with Junior, and I am sure she is still harboring a lot of emotional pain in her anger of loss. The same goes for Judy, the eldest of Junior's maternal aunts, whose love and well wishes for all her children cannot be overemphasized. Judy and I grew up together in Christian youth camps, and I know her uniqueness in family values and happiness—a quality which I also tried to pass on to my boy. All the women in Junior's life, though in this pain of loss must now learn to accept the fact that it was God's will for him to leave us in his youth. I am quite sure that God must have given him a great new assignment in the kingdom of heaven.

The Berman and Pollack names had become familiar names in the Mbeng household for over two decades, so in their rights, Lea and Diane were also women in Junior's life. They both attended his viewing and funeral service, respectively. On a trip home from Los Angeles, I presented this script to Mrs. B (Lea), and she said the sentimental expressions were very powerful—an opinion that left some smiles on my face as we drove down 66 from IAD. Lea and Wayne, a.k.a. Mr. and Mrs. Berman, were my special friends and clients for so many years, and we had been raising our kids with identical moral concerns. This was true for Mr. and Mrs. Pollack too. I am quite certain that their visits to the Fairfax Memorial Park Funeral Home on those fateful July days were visits that they all would rather have liked to miss, and I can say with utmost certainty that Junior appreciated their presence very much, and I obviously did too.

Martha. She was quite fond of me, and she, Rose, and I never ceased to recite lines from Shakespeare's work, and we were all very good at it. Martha is so brilliantly poetic and uses this talent to dissuade me from the agony of my son's passing, just by putting appropriate words together; and even though she and Junior didn't visit much, she cared about him, just like everyone else, and has since made sure that the stringent sad feelings of the melancholy flee from my constant well-being.

I like to conclude this chapter with an outing from Mary Yen Njoka, my elementary and secondary school sweetheart's sister. Mary lost her son a few years back in Chicago, Illinois, but has not recovered from her loss because parents don't recover from the loss of a child, as my secondary school literature teacher, Mr. Sammy Arrey-Mbi, articulated when I called to condole with him about the loss of his daughter just months after my ordeal. In her words Mary wrote the following:

Dealing with the pain of losing a child

Dear K, I am sorry for the delay in sending this to you. It's been quite hectic with work, and the holidays have put a damper on writing and sending this to you. Here we go: Since Laimo passed away, my life has not been the same. How can it be the same when a child who gave me the taste of motherhood is not here? Sometimes I sit staring at the door, waiting for that deep voice of his to say, "Reme open next door." It is such an ere feeling, but it is the truth. After telling my story for so long, and when the tears did not flow anymore, I knew I was finally healing. I am still

plagued by constant fears though, that this could happen again as I call my youngest son, Aaron to check on him every time he goes out with friends. I am glad you are putting our stories out there for the public to know what we sometimes take for granted. Thank you for doing so my dear! Yen.

Typical Mary! I was beat when her son went to meet his maker, but only truly realized her pain when mine too slept away into eternity. Her bravery in handling her emotions of pain has been remarkable, and she is one in this our unique club of parents who mourn to draw strength from, for even the scriptures teach us that blessed are those who mourn, for they shall be comforted. So comfort, there shall be!

CHAPTER ELEVEN

A LETTER FROM A FATHER
TO A DEPARTED SON

My dear son,

Writing a letter to a son should be one of the greatest pleasures of life in the life of a father, but I am writing to you today in destitute, in painful thought, and with desperate imaginations, since all I know I am doing is expressing my feelings, not knowing how I will deliver these words of adulation to you. It seems like just yesterday, but one year has gone by without your presence in any way, shape, or form. Trips to your room have not relented, and the monitoring of the doors late at night is still a practical phenomenon, with empty imaginations that you could walk through someday, even though the possibility of that not happening is crystal-clear—particularly because it was I who sealed your coffin and filled the grave. I still cannot understand why this had to happen to me, and it is terribly agonizing to think that it did; and this too goes for everybody in the family.

People have been asking me so many questions about what could have gone wrong, or maybe right, since no one knows and understands the Will of God. I too have been asking myself the same questions and have realized that asking them is counter-productive, for there will never be right answers to share. What I know and believe is that you are now in a good resting place, probably doing what you wish to do, as God allows you to. When you were here with us, we took so many things for granted and made so many assumptions about the time we have under our control here on earth. It is now evidently clear to me, and many others, that we do not have the luxury of time to do all the things that we plan to do, which is why I have all these regrets about what you, Taku, and I could have been doing, rather than wasting all the energy rattling and wrangling on unproductive procrastinations.

Before I continue with our relationship concerns, I wish to know if you have already met with my parents and siblings who went before you. Do they recognize you—for those who knew you here on earth—and is there a way to keep in touch with you all in heaven, even if it is just to receive signals about our curiosities?

Back to you and me: That Friday afternoon that you came to my room to complain about your ears has recycled on my mind, over and over again, with wishes of the hope that I could get clear understanding of what I needed to do to avert such a catastrophic end. I want you to know now as you must have known then, that your health and Taku's were always a priority to us, which is why your mother and I were so concerned about your plight in the first place. She reports well right now, but every now and then, tears run down her eyes in memory of the joy she should have been having with you around, and I am sure you can find ways up there to signal to her some productive ways that would ease her pain of loss. Taku still does not talk much as you already know, and is visibly shaken whenever the subject of your departure comes up. It may be great if you can send signals or reach him too. He was your best friend—Remember?

In retrospect, I can't stop remembering the good old days, when my boys (you and Taku) jumped on each other, ate together, went to football practices together, played Xboxes together, doing all the fun things together that brothers do. I remember how you used to drag Taku around the neighborhood in Manassas and Woodbridge under the rains, and how I would drive down on every neighborhood street trying to find you guys. That was the joy of being a parent, even though some yelling was involved; and I now miss even the yelling, since Taku is still the cool type that you know. Sometimes, we parents feel like it is our responsibility to choose and advise on career choices for our children; and we sometimes do so by ignoring their personal desires and relative ambitions. I must say I am very guilty of this discrepancy, for I know I was pushing you very hard on what I wanted you to be, but not listening attentively to what you wanted to be. I truly wish I could do this all over again, and I am now using your example on handling your brother's freedom of choices—knowing that this would give you some satisfaction wherever you are. I am also publishing my absolute experience of your sudden departure for my readers to learn from it, particularly the parents who are still taking things for granted as I did. Even some kids need to learn from it too. I sing this song below to you every time I visit your grave, and it is a favorite of your grandfather's too, so share the words with him if there is congregation for you all up there where you are:

WHEN WE ALL GET TO HEAVEN
Eliza E. Hewitt

1. Sing the wondrous love of Jesus
Sing His Mercy and His Grace
In the Mansions bright and Blessed
He'll prepare for us a Place.

REFRAIN: When we all get to Heaven,
What a Day of rejoicing that will be!
When we all see Jesus
We'll sing and shout the victory!

2. While we walk the pilgrim pathway
Clouds will overspread the sky
But when the trav'lling days are over,
Not a shadow, not a sigh.

3. Let us then be true and faithful
Trusting, serving every day;
Just one glimpse of Him in glory'
Will the toils of life repay

PRINCE KAFAIN EMMANUEL MBENG, SR.

4. Onward to the prize before us!
Soon His beauty we'll behold;
Soon the pearly gates will open,
We shall tread the streets of gold

My boy, no day goes by without the thought of you, and I am sure this is how it will now be for the rest of my life. That last father's day that you and your brother spoiled me with delicious dining at that fancy "All you can eat" restaurant in Tyson's Corner will also remain passionate in my mind, especially since it was the day that you showed maturity and responsibility by informing me that you had gotten Taku a job where you were working. Of course, he didn't end up picking up the job, since you left two days before his starting date, but your badge and his are hanging on my memorial wall as a reminder of your productive effort. Someone came to bid you fare-well from your workplace, and I am sure he was either the manager there or your supervisor. Could tell he was quite saddened too.

Down here on earth, we spend so much time lamenting on so many things that we wish we could do or attain, and of course, your memory of what I am saying is still fresh since it wasn't too long ago that you were here. And it is always our wish to know whether such lamentation happens up there too, or whether people up there have the same kind of experiences that we go through down here. To me these thoughts are hypothetical, because my four sisters who went up before you, and particularly Aunt Angeline, would have sent me word or caused me to have some understanding on what to expect from here. The mystery will certainly live on, until I join you there; and maybe you'll be older and assigned to coach me as a new kid on the block. It would be interesting to know, and if that were actually to happen, it would be fun reversing positions with you, and having you in heaven as my dad, and your grandpa as my grandfather, and the same goes for grandma.

You still remember Professor Nelson Ngoh in Bridgeport, Connecticut—right? The uncle who used to call you "Chuck Norris," and say you had very entertaining talents! He came down for your funeral and got quite emotionally concerned when he and I seriously reflected on our inability to stop your sudden departure. "Bo Junior," he called out to me. "This child is too young to die *naa*," he added in tears. I am bringing him up because, after November 2001, when his wife also departed to be with the Lord, he decided to write her a letter—just as I am now doing. We both agreed on its publication as our way of raising awareness in our communities about cancer, which was what took her life, and the lamentations he made in his letter were exceedingly marvelous. His expressions in his work were quite prolific and precise, and I am sure he felt very good knowing that he had done his best in his attempt to save Agnes's life. He never told me whether or not a reply ever came back, and neither have I ever asked him. His lamentation concept seemed strange to me at the time, but when I decided to include a letter to you in this memoir or book of memory, I thought of Bo Makwen, as I fondly call him, and how he would enjoy the fact that I am emulating this his unique concept. It is important to note that Nelson was there for me when I too was diagnosed with prostate cancer, and has comfortably quoted my cancer book, *Cancer Diagnosis is Not a Death Sentence* on several of his personal and professional discussions.

Watching the evening news has not gotten any easier for me, and for Taku too, for there is some story on substance abuse or some kind of overdose awareness report, concerning adult kids about your age and in all walks—of life almost every night. We have news stories on OPIOID crisis plaguing our communities; we have news stories about overdose uses of fentanyl, OxyContin, and oxycodone, and many more. I am only now learning that there is a reversal drug called naloxone, but this new knowledge won't be any useful now, if that's what I had needed for you. To this day, this fact perturbs my preventive imagination. These stories always hit me hard and make me uncomfortable, since the toxicology report which we received indicated fentanyl intoxication, a drug that I had never before then heard of. I wish, hope, and pray that this drug problem can be contained. Lamenting on it now does me no good, nor serves me no purpose, except to leave me in pain and more pain—assuming that that was what happened since I can't get your take on this now. But I have chosen to stay sane and positive, in order to protect your brother and all others wherever I could have failed you. It is with great difficulty that I do this though, but the peaceful way in which things unfolded on that fateful evening gives me solace to believe that you have peace of mind in your new and permanent home.

My boy, Every now and then, I am still mentally tortured and affected by the incident that I heard occurred at your friend's home when, as you said, you were upstairs sleeping, and I still wish to know more about what had actually happened even if it's just for general knowledge. The story of your girlfriend's cousin continues to plague my mind; it was frightening then and still frightens me now and definitely must have contributed to my ineptness to participate in the proceedings that followed, especially when your counsel refused to discuss any details with me. It is obvious that this bothered you too, and I understand perfectly well why it would have been difficult for you to fill me in, and wish we had had a memorandum of understanding about this issue when it happened. It is too late now, and knowing the details now will be obsolete and pointless, but I want you to rest assured that I harbor no hard feelings on the incident.

On a lighter note, son, your birthday comes up in just a few days, September 7, 1993, and your brother is planning a private memorial with me, your mother, and some very close family and friends, just as we did two months ago on July 14—the day we rested you in peace. My numerous visits to your grave have given me, and I think all of us, enormous courage to be able to deal with our xenophobic feelings whenever we choose to do anything significant; and it would be comforting to have some signals from you on that day if you if you can. I intend to bring down Victoria and her brothers, so they too can be able to express and share their uplifting memories, and I know you will be smiling down on us. Give us some inspirational signals on that day if you can.

Today, September 7, 2019, is or would have been your twenty-sixth birthday, and the original plan for celebration has been adjusted to include Uncle Kakwah's visit. Yes! You were born in Detroit, Michigan, where Uncle Kakwah and Aunty Nain lived at the time. They and your mother had become very close after their wedding in the Cameroons, which is how the plan to deliver you in

Michigan got hatched. Uncle Kakwah, aunties Nain and Delphine, and I have just returned home from some manifestations at your grave. That is how we now celebrate you, and I am sure that your uncle/godfather will be expressing his personal feelings to you himself, when he too decides to pen-in. You know you were so special to so many people in the family, and Uncle Kakwah says he still remembers—just like it was yesterday—your conversation with him on that Father's Day—two weeks before he lost you. The thought of your untimely departure is killing his good spirits, and I could not help to notice how devastated his emotions were tearing him down, when I handed over my letter to you for him to read out. Aunty Nain knelt on the grave speechless, while listening attentively as your uncle read the script to you, and we all acted as if your presence was true to life, especially since there was no way of knowing your reactions from the other side. We then retired into a long evening, but the numerous activities did not take away your memories in my head, and most likely, everyone else's. Uncles Patrice, Larry, Gilbert, and their wives had joined us for the evening to celebrate that special day, even though not everyone might have been reflecting about you the same way.

This writing exercise has not only been difficult for me; it has been extremely difficult for your brother too, and after feeling reluctant to yield to this strange request, he has finally mustered the courage to drop a few lines to you below:

> *Dear Jr, Summer was at its peak, and it was a humid and emotional day for our family at Fairfax Memorial Funeral Home. Funerals are common, and almost everybody experiences one somehow in his or her family, but it never occurred to me that I could be so involved in one so soon. I have always thought about you and I planning funerals for Daddy and Mommy, but not the other way round. It has taken me until now to realize that when you lose someone this close, you wake up one day, and nothing seems*

normal in your world again. Looking back at that terrible day, I still can't understand why something like this would happen to me at a time when you and I were just beginning to enjoy our lives together as young adults. I am baffled by this thought every day, and it frustrates me to think that you are permanently gone. You were my big brother and best friend, and your death has created a vacuum that I will live with for the rest of my life. But Daddy and Mommy encourage me all the time to have more understanding of what to expect in life. We have no control over our time here on earth, Dad keeps repeating, and all we do now is pay frequent visits to your grave hoping you can see or hear us when we come.

Just weeks before Daddy and I rushed in to your room to try to revive you from whatever overdose you had taken, everything in your life was finally falling in place. You were finally getting your life together piece by piece and taking up on bigger responsibilities, like being on your own phone plan, getting a good-paying job, planning to find your own place where you could live freely, and even though it was common for people your age, twenty-five, to make imperfect choices, you seemed to be on the right path. You were always the "social butterfly," who knew how to interact with any and everybody. It is extremely difficult for me to believe that you are just a story of memory now, and I will make sure that I keep this story and memory alive until we meet again. Love!

Your brother,
Taku

As you yourself can see, Taku's writing skills have improved greatly, and he now expresses himself well in script too—just like you know who! I told him that this memoir would eventually serve him well, in the many years to come, when he may need to remember stories about you to tell his kids and grandkids. I am sure you agree with me on this suggestion, right? Whether or not you do, our resolve to stay positively reflective on you remains the same, and our message about your days here on earth will always remain the same and unchanged.

My friend, your other godfather, Uncle Danny was just with me on the phone a few moments ago, wishing you were still around to register for a scrum master course that will yield you a six-figure salary. This would have been perfect for you, and my joke about living in your basement someday might have come even faster than I thought. (Danny was one of three godfathers for both my boys who received baptism on the same day.) I added your brother to the call, and he was coached on what to do to complete the course and receive certification if he is interested, and I just thought I throw this back at you, so you can guide him, maybe, from upstairs, assuming it is practically possible.

When you were a toddler, your doctor was my friend and brother-in-law, Dr. Asek Makia, the doctor who always gave you the pink medicine that you later said tasted good. Dr. Makia came to the house when he heard the news. Uncle Abdul, a.k.a. John, Yoti and Namei's dad, also came, not forgetting the Okangs—remember Aunty Eli, uncle Njabu's sister in Ellicott City, Maryland, and her husband, Dr. Uncle George. They too were here and very sad about your passing, and Aunty Eli was pleased to hear that I was burying you next to her brother. Aunty Pauline says Papa Tee has moved to California, Los Angeles, I think. The list of family and friends who still ask about you every time they run into me is so long that I can't even begin to name them to you. You were a great kid with great connections, and a starlet in your rights, just like your dad in his youthful days, but you couldn't live to explore these benefits; maybe that's what God wanted for you, and who knows what you are where you are right now?

CHAPTER TWELVE

OVERCOMING THE
CHALLENGES OF THE LOSS

The desire to trade places with my son continues to be an understatement as I ponder ceaselessly on this consequential challenge in my life that has fortified my premonition on emotional security. The study of death or dying—thanatology—has gained prevalence in recent years, and my guess is that the understanding and acceptance is no longer principally the concern of poets only, but a societal infectious norm that we all are subjected and exposed to. Understanding the emotional setbacks of such devastating losses is challenging, but at the same time, parents and other mourners must analyze the circumstances surrounding their loss in order to vindicate themselves from associated painful and constant reflections. Overcoming the challenges of the loss of my son will be my main focus in this chapter, even though an attempt to generalize the experience and recommendations will be significantly noted.

A family is made up of a father, a mother, brothers, and sisters, and this unit extends to include uncles, aunts, cousins, close friends, and many more. All these relatives are usually equally affected by the loss of anyone in the family, and the pain they share is often immeasurable. Keeping them bonded during such times is of utmost importance, and any lapse in doing so could result in other unforeseen contingencies that would require even more attention. In my case, I knew I had to take immediate control of the grieving process and literally dictate when and how to grieve, even though outbursts of emotions were frequently unstoppable. My brother and his family had moved into my house to run domestic matters, and family and friends were constantly coming in and out, or on their phones, expressing consolations and opinions about what they thought needed to be done as we initiated the funeral plans.

Having to explain my thought process, and every action I was taking about the ordeal, was becoming quite challenging to my daily routines, especially at home where all my emotional sentiments would always be associated with the loss. When one is married and builds a strong and loving family, the vulnerability of losing everything he has accumulated over the years becomes risky, if for any reason this family starts to disintegrate. The challenge to hold things together and the reaction of the kids becomes a serious concern that could debilitate into some ugly condition. The thought of such a consequence lived in my head since June of 2012, when our family bond was broken, and all that followed conjectured into lots of disparaging scenarios for our boys. I had tried to do all that I could do to retain some sanity and leave them out of my melancholies, but they were part of the family and were definitely bound to suffer consequentially. As the senior son, Junior took upon himself to step up and try to be the man of the house, but his efforts came with lots of shortfalls, given all the dependencies involved, in alliance with his inexperience on sentimental domestic issues.

I now feel terrible and responsible for this unforeseen disintegration—the guilt of which gives me uncomfortable chills. But the responsible behavior and way which his brother is comporting himself restores my courage and hope, taking away most of my cultivated guilt, since I am truly confident that nothing I did had malicious intent. To be clear, the art of creative writing has been therapeutic enough for me, and in spite of recommendations made by the National Cancer Institute and the American Psychological Association on cognitive behavioral therapy, I have ruled out expensive professional therapy sessions for my boy and myself during this bereavement period.

THE FEAR FACTOR: Despite my willingness to move on, simple things anger and frighten me every day. I am home alone whenever I'm not at work, and this goes for Taku and Delphine, when they too are not performing the normal routines of school and work, respectively. There is always the fear that something could happen when any one of us is home alone, and I am constantly walking to Taku's room to ensure that he is there and doing well, especially when he doesn't respond to my shoutouts. I even worry when I lock my bathroom door, with constant fears that help would be far if something unexpected were to happen. This fear is generally common, but after bereavement, it becomes relatively difficult to overcome such fear, or "watch the paint dry," as Robin on the *Howard Stern Show* would say. The challenge itself is challenging; some days, all you can do is cry, try to sleep, wake up with insomnia, and cry some more. Sleep deprivation is usually common at this stage, and mood swings accompany sentiments and emotional displays. After six months to a year, you hope all these symptoms will go away, but every thought and reflection of your loss rejuvenates bereavement again. You get depressed and annoyed about everything and everyone, even when nothing has happened during the hard day, and the fear of being crazy starts to set in; but all you need to do is to remember that you are dealing with an unchangeable situation, and no matter the circumstance, nothing you do can change the outcome of this circumstance. I am sure that the line to heaven would have been jammed, if we knew how to reach God's secretary, but I believe even hell doesn't take calls from earth. Which is why I tell my boy and all in my house to accept the reality of it and make fun of the good memories we had with our loved one, for that's all we will ever have left.

If you depended on your child or loved one for financial support, the challenge to overcome his or her loss becomes even greater to bear, especially if you had to use credit cards to cover funeral costs. Billing cycles become annoying and convoluted with complaints and fury, making collectors to become inconveniencing enemies, even when they know nothing about what happened to you. On a positive note, take a moment to reflect on associate behavior by asking your-self some simple pertinent questions such as the following:

1. Do I really owe these people?
2. Can I afford to settle these debts?
3. If I was a creditor and someone owed me, would I not want my money back?
4. Did my loss take away my natural decency and responsibility?

These simple questions will call your psyche to order, for we can overcome every challenge differently and with integrity. Emptiness and loneliness are just realistic characteristics, and an attempt to break out from them by socializing more would definitely help any-one trying to overcome the challenge of loss.

Parents need to automatically have full rights to collect and assess information about their children from doctors, teachers, law-yers, etc., in most circumstances, for they are the ones who face the challenges of grooming and identifying their behavioral follies. Who knows if this right, which I was denied each time I tried to intervene on some important predicament in my son's life, was a key factor in my ordeal? We may never know, even though knowing now adds nothing to my emotional challenges. Trying to overcome loss is also challenging in arousing a sense of injustice in relation to fear, pain, and deep sadness, and, in some cases, suicidal thoughts enter into a parent's head, as a result of shame, guilt, and the stigma of rejec-tion. When these symptoms start surfacing, it is important to look into cognitive behavioral therapy (CBT) as recommended by the American Psychological Institute. We can't avoid the pain of loss, yet millions blame themselves and try to run away from it. There is a sweet side to loss, which is that it opens one's pain to joy and reconstruction—depending on the willingness to overcome all these associated challenges.

In most cultures, and particularly the African culture, the first-born male child in every family setting is usually always ready to step in to assume responsibility when his father becomes absent either by death or for any other reason; and I can say with certainty that my son, Junior, was bravely challenged when our family unit collapsed in 2012. On several occasions, I had to remind him that I was still going to be there for all of them, and that my main concern was for them to receive a good education and be able to live a comfortable life when I was gone. Needless to indicate my experiences on similar issues in my childhood that made me step in to protect my sisters. But my situation was temporary, and quickly came to an end in a truly compromising fashion. Reflections on these experiences and the imagination that a child could be living in fear of such feelings of depression is extremely challenging—the outcome of which could lead to a rise in anxiety and acute depression. That was my fear then, and continues to be my fear now, and the fear of so many other parents in my circles, the remedy of which cannot clearly be defined than to say—we should keep doing what we know is right all the time, and leave the rest in the Hands of the Lord.

The effects of the loss of a dear one could remain dormant for many years but resurface again powerfully in a significant memorial encounter. This is what makes it relatively challenging to overcome the pain and emotions of loss.

A MAGICAL MOMENT: The Ghanghas, Chris, and I had just returned to their residence after the Celestine Waindim viewing, and as I sat down on the couch to relax and meditate, my eyes immediately landed on the face of one beautiful young lady, who looked so familiar even though I knew I had never seen her before. Something about her was strikingly memorable, and even the stare in her eyes drew some strange strong feelings within me; so I wanted so much to know who she was, at the same time beginning to wonder why her looks were affecting me the way they did. So I asked to know who she was and was almost blown away when the name Angeline Nkwain was mentioned. Her name is Judith, she is married to Genesis, they have two beautiful kids. And yes! She is a photocopy of her mother, Angeline Nkwain. Angeline was my teenage sweetheart after high school, and the reason we didn't marry then was because we were both so young and couldn't support life on our own. That would be some forty-five-plus years ago, and her passing in 2000 was quite a shock to my imagination on what life she and I could have grown into. I am sure we both enjoyed the lives that God blessed us with, nonetheless!

Coping with the loss of a loved one was quite a challenge and still is. It is a difficult challenge, but little memories and reflections of our departed loved ones help to ease the pain of loss and provide hope and courage to move on. Meeting Angeline's daughter became a perfect distraction for my emotions throughout my stay in Minnesota, and the reciprocal reaction and extension of our connection to her sister, Rose Mary, in the Cameroons gave me instant pleasure. Angeline had once told me when one of my rivals mocked at me on educational aptitude that "hurt people hurt people," an expression that I thought was too advanced for her level, but that must have been her developmental benefit from working with English Reverend sisters at St. Bedes College in Ashing, Kom. If only my learned friend knew that I was one of only two A-Level candidates with the highest score in history in January of 1977. My brother Kakwah thought that night's excitement was strange when my predicaments became the highlight of our socialization in my hotel suite, with Foinchas's narrative of past "Angeline" memories adding to the fun. We can undoubtedly use the good memories of our loved ones as a coping mechanism to deal with our emotional frustrations, which of course was the situation in which I found myself as I continued to lament on the fact that God would choose to call my son first, and not me.

A PEDAGOGIC FLASHBACK
OF JUNIOR'S GRANDPA

As already stated in the introduction, my father, Johnson Mbeng, took over the administration of Baptist schools in the British Southern Cameroons from Evan's dad, Dr. Gilbert Schneider. Dr. Schneider was an intelligent, good-hearted, foresighted, kind, and benevolent American missionary, who came to the Southern Cameroons (now called Ambazonia) as a visionary and true missionary servant of God. Gilbert and Johnson had so much in common in their philosophies of life, and their personalities never conflicted in any way, shape, or form, particularly in their beliefs in education and pedagogy. They both raised their kids to reflect these beliefs, in hope that they would emulate these beliefs and did much within their powers to improve upon the existing substandard system of education and culture in the grasslands of the Cameroons.

It is important to note that they initiated the opening of the Mbingo Baptist hospital, in collaboration with Dr. Paul Gebauer— one of the founding fathers of Baptist missions in the Cameroons. It was Dr. Gebauer who incidentally chose my mother as the lead Baptist girl that they took around communities, in order to attract girls like her to the school. It was also Dr. Gebauer who brought over my dad from the government or the Native Authority administration, and then obliged him to convert from Presbyterian to Baptist if he wanted my mother's hand in marriage. My mother, Mary, and

Evan's mother, Mildred (all blessed memories), would thus become Christian sisters—breaking some of the primitive barriers of the times.

It is also important to note the instrumental roles both Johnson Mbeng and Gilbert Schneider played in the discovery of the stolen statue of Kom, popularly known as "Afo A Kom," and the facilitation of the return of this statue from the African Art Museum at the Smithsonian in Washington DC to the Kom Fondom in the early seventies. Its arrival at the Bali airport was a distinguished diplomatic affair, and so many people have wanted to claim credit for this discovery and diplomacy over the years. Details of this would totally be a different topic for discussion because of these controversial acclamations.

Evan Schneider did call me when my son, Junior suddenly passed and was concerned and interested in the cause of death. With our Christian background, he knew how we had been raised and could not imagine, I believe, and rightly so, that our son would be victim to the OPIOID crisis that was inherently plaguing our nation and the world at large. I was probably so overwhelmed with the shock of death to remember to call him after the toxicology report came in; and I am just now confirming his worst fear. In this chapter, I am going to defer commentary on our parents' pedagogic sentiment to him, in hope that it will be a good opportunity for him to revisit his affiliations in the Cameroons, notwithstanding general interests on his views relating to pedagogy and child loss, or even the Mbingo projects.

This is Evan…"There is a saying that if you ask questions, you will be lost." I like this idea because to be curious and ask questions will help me discover more about life. I know Pa Johnson and Pa Gilbert had many questions and enjoyed talking far into the night sometimes enjoying roasted chicken rubbed in salt and palm oil. Their examples gave me a sense

that questions were a key that opened the doors to stories of connection.

Pa Gilbert loved Kom and was never tired of taking photographs of the people, celebrations, architecture, and landscape of this beautiful place. I know this place reminded him of his birthplace in the Willamette Valley, Oregon. The rich volcanic soils, waterfalls, and family farms he grew up on were uniquely suited to starting a 23 square mile, self-sufficient leprosy settlement at Mbingo. The settlement had patients from all over Cameroon who had been shunned by their families due to the incurable disease they now carried. A cure was eventually developed however, but many of the patients remained at Mbingo because few others were skeptical that they were actually cured, when they saw their missing fingers and toes as a result of the leprosy.

In addition to physical healing, there was also need to restore the creative energy that could make them whole again. Gilbert started inviting artist to work on internship basis, to teach and inspire the patients. Robert Toh, a wood carver from Babanki, and Umaru Njasi, a brass caster from Bamenda joined a painter from Nigeria, a raffia weaver from Ndop, and many others over the years. The handicraft tradition of patients making saleable artifacts continues to this day.

There was also a close relationship that developed between Pa Gilbert and the Fons of Kom. Fon Ndi, Fon Looh, and Fon Nsom were all people he respected. When the royal palace at Laikom burned, he helped rebuild it, and when the Afo A Kom was missing from the palace, Gilbert Schneider helped Johnson Mbeng and Evan Schneider work on a plan with others to return it to Laikom. It had been located in the museum in Washington. From the time Mbingo opened in 1952 to his death in 1999, Gilbert's interest and love of Kom never wavered. He and Johnson corresponded and detailed Kom history and culture over decades.

Pa Gilbert was nicknamed as Masa Toroki. A name given because people said he was at home where ever he went. This legacy has made me want to ask my own questions too, so that I will never be lost.

I am so sad to say I never met Junior... but I will never forget him. Because Junior was Johnson's grandson means he was Gilbert's grandson too. Because he was Kafain's son means he was my son too. Kafain's brother is named Gilbert after my father, and Kafain's nephew is named Evan after me. We are still a unique family the way Gilbert and Johnson, and Mildred and Mary would want. Kafain doesn't like flying, and we have five thousand miles separating us, which must be why he didn't bring Junior and his brother to visit us. But as he has rightly said, it was the Will of God that he left us at such a young age, and he is surely resting in a better place. We will continue to keep his photographs and memories alive. It is a terrible thing to loss a child though, and I pray every day for Kafain—the Prince of Kom after his father.

Evan Schneider

Dr. Gilbert **Schneider** and his friend Bobe Johnson **Mbeng** in
a moment of reunion and excitement in the early nineties.

These two were like brothers and always played like kids and
kept a remarkable relation until their deaths.

Dr. Schneider was very much part of my life when he learned
from my dad that I had finally made it to the US for further studies.
He immediately contacted me and started sending me material information about the work that he and my father did in the Cameroons.
He told me so many stories that I didn't know and debunked some
theories on misinformation about so many things that transpired
during his time there. I would only then learn from him that he
wanted my dad to move his family to the States when he foresaw the
consequences of the new wave of neocolonialism in West Cameroon.
But my father's princely mentality wouldn't let him abandon his
extended family and tribe, even if it meant seeking the glories of

a better life abroad. That was my dad, as I knew him through the eyes of his bosom friend, and my son, Junior, would come to admire the convictions of his grandfather more in pictures and tales than in person. With very little knowledge of his grandfather's life history, Junior always told me he wanted to be like him when he grew up— an expression of a wish that will now never be achieved.

CHAPTER FOURTEEN

CONCLUSION

You have just lost a child and gone through the preliminary mourning process of wakes, funeral, visitations, and solitaries. Your mind is still set on the heavenly kingdom, where everyone claims your boy is gone to, and then you start to reflect on the Bible verse in which Jesus says, "In my father's house, there are many mansions, if it were not so, I would have told you. I go to prepare a place for you, and when I have prepared the place, I will come again."

Then in the same light, you remember the verse in Matthews 5 that says, "Blessed are those who mourn, for they shall be comforted." All the comfort of loss that needed to come your way has already come and gone, and consolation has returned to normalcy. The anger in you is still there, and your expression of it is moderately understandable. Your life is supposed to reshape and move on, but that would be very unrealistic. You then enter into the grieving process and seek redemption from every angle. Your sister and your brother are not there enough, and this drives you really crazy; especially because you remember all you believe you gave up to get them where they are. Your silence wakes up every morning with disillusionment about something in life that is wrong and affecting you directly or even indirectly. You call out to all who know you are grieving, but the answers are all the same. People seem to have moved on and hope you would too. Then you remember all the promises everyone made when you were mourning, about reaching out any-

136

time for anything. And the understanding of the truisms of life begin to set in rapidly. You make empty declarations and decide to sit alone in your own world, without interference from the outside world; but this too only worsens your emotional pain, drawing you back to a few people in your circle of family and friends. Confusion about who really cares about you and your well-being scrambles on your mind, and you begin to realize that some of your enemies may actually have been your friends, but for the discrepancies. You get tired hearing the phrase "I am so sorry for your loss," such that you almost want to repeat it or say it too before the next consoler finishes up. Psychologists and religious personalities have pondered on this subject many times in their lectures and consultations and arrived at a conclusion, I believe, that there is no clear-cut solution to this myth. Every case is different, and finding a conventional solution is a waste of time. For every case is different!

The fact that my son was dead and buried will never change, and even though his loss has ramshackled my world and caused my family and me everlasting pain, the choice to accept our fate and move on cannot be overstated. Memories of him will live in us forever, and we will continue to pay visits to his grave and place flowers on it whenever we do. That is all we can now do. This is actually nothing anyone should cherish doing in his or her lifetime, but doing it gives families a sort of relief that only they can relate to and/or explain.

After expressing a solid perspective on the issues that I have tried to raise and address in this memoir, it will be needless for me to rewrite the details again. However, I must reiterate and emphasize the importance of not worrying about the things in one's life that are beyond his or her control, and which he or she cannot change—a motto of life since my childhood that my father always approved. I always consulted with him on everything that could affect my life, and he told me when I had grown up that my philosophy of life had finally paid off in the way I was handling crucial and delicate family matters. I felt good hearing so from a trusted authority, and glorified on it, even if some imperfections existed.

Watching evening news was not so common when I was growing up as a kid because we didn't have television where I was, and radios were principally reserved for our fathers, who always had a monopoly over them. But today, the first thing everyone (including kids) do when we enter the house is to turn on the TV. The evening news is always about crime and politics, and there is crime everywhere! One thing responsible for the increase in crime rate is the illegal drug sales and consumption. Many young people are often attracted to these drugs by either the money or recreation effect; and sooner than later, they become addicted. "Do not get into a lion's den, even if it is sleeping; for getting in there is always easier than getting out," I often told my boys. Once kids get into the drug market and then start living the resulting lifestyles, they never find it easy to quit, and those who try face all kinds of challenges from hooking up in the first place. I watched one report on ABC News that was focused on people's fear of being labelled "a snitch" when they find themselves caught up with these illegal drug activities, and then they try to cooperate with law enforcement—the consequence of which always results in becoming criminals and/or victims of crime.

Parents need to be aware of such eventualities and must have discussions with their children lest they find themselves in some kind of limbo. The task is difficult though, especially when they unfortunately have little or no knowledge of what these kids could be doing, but having a good relationship and conversation with them all the time, gives you the satisfaction that you are doing your best. What happens after that will happen no matter what! I undoubtedly had a good relationship with my boy, but I guess it wasn't good enough to save him from drug overdose; and if this can happen to me, it can happen to you too.

I won't actually be certain that I have succeeded to enlighten anyone about the nightmare that stems from losing a child until I get feedback from my readers. However, I can say with some degree of certainty that trying to relay these thoughts with little or no embellishment has preoccupied my mind enough to have me decompressed from most of my emotional setbacks. The loss of a child has become a club to some of us as my beloved Yen-Marie rightly ascertains, and a noble and distinguished one too, for only the bravest of the brave can withstand the elusions of the sudden death syndrome to be able to smile, and smile again with everlasting tears in your eyes. Junior and all the departed children were all very fine people—and must still be very fine people wherever they are now. Even though we continue to love them dearly, we must—yes *must*—let them go, and maybe they might just be speaking for us in heaven.

Mindful of all the shortcomings of that fateful day that has become a day of reckoning and apprehension in my family, and mindful of all the consequences brought upon us by a sudden and tragic miscalculation,

Mindful of the challenges of overcoming the loss of a child, and mindful of the constant fears and parental awareness difficulties.

Mindful of the desperate rants by a desolate father in his resolve to be courageous for the strength and goodness of the rest of his family, and mindful of the perspectives of his mother and all the women in his life.

Mindful of community responsibility on preventive measures to abate the coping of the loss of a dear one, and mindful of all the lessons learned from the loss and the financial concerns on contingent preparedness.

The loss of a child will continue to remain one of the most, if not the most, terrible thing to happen to any parent in his or her lifetime. It is therefore with much disdain that I choose to embark on this honest declaration, with the hope that many would learn from my example and be able to avert any such unforeseen contingency that could befall them too. May God bless you!

ACKNOWLEDGMENTS

Hon. Wayne Berman of BE and the BLACKSTONE GROUP and Mr. Rick Pollack, CEO of AHA are like brothers to me, and they have both been quite instrumental to the success of my business venture. The three of us are about the same age, and their loyalties to me as my priority executive clients for over a quarter of a century have brought prosperity to my business. Their wives—Lea and Diane, respectively—have also enhanced a perfect friendly atmosphere for me over all these years. It was a great honor to my family and me for all of them to take time off their busy schedules to attend Junior's wake and funeral services, and I want them to know that I am very grateful. I acknowledge and thank them individually, for patronizing my executive transportation services and encouraging my skills and perfection in business management consulting. There is no greatness in business greater than learning from the best! Many others in my professional life such as Tom Nickels, Marc Cohen, Peggy Vasquez, Barb Henry, Shami Scott, Darlene Vanderbush, Crystal Childs, and Carla Brown are all also acknowledged for their cooperation in different areas. Chris Chiatoh, my deputy, deserves special recognition for staying with me for years under all circumstances.

Everyone in my family is acknowledged, with special appreciation to all those who in every way, shape, or form enabled the smoothness of Junior's farewell celebration. There is no doubt on my mind that you all came morally, emotionally, financially, and spiritually. God bless all of you! Again, to my son, Taku, I simply have to say, thank you for your support and cooperation—cooperation that has held me together and turned the emotions of my pain into the emotions of hope. It is important to note here that all the photographic and technical work for this edition came through with Taku's direction, which of course makes his integral contribution to the entire production commendable. Dr. Joseph Ngeh Toyang has also provided encouragement and has taken time off his cancer research work to write the preface for this publication. Just like his father, Evan Schneider has always demonstrated concern and come through every time I ask him to do me a favor. That is how we were able to redeem Gilbert from the torture at home. For that, and for his interest in my work, I am absolutely very grateful.

To Victor and Elsie, Junior's other parents, their passion and affection for all our six Alexandria, Virginia, kids—and my Junior in particular—will never be overstated, even when our indifferent actions could have been misconstrued in a stream of thoughts of desperation. Their meaningful intentions have forever remained in appreciation. Ka and I go a long way back, to Douala and the Chiabi compound, and as brothers, an attitude of brotherhood, friendship, and responsibility has always been fostered during good and bad times, and this attitude was also practically visibly demonstrated during this sad episode of our lives. Visi and Nain couldn't have made a more meaningful representation.

No! I didn't single Ka out, and no, I didn't forget the family: All the Taku Chiabi kids, grandkids, and great-grandkids were notoriously present in their respective rights and capacities—no qualms, and I must say, I am truly grateful. To the Mbeng clan under my distinguished and undisputed leadership, self-praise and gratification will remain silent at this time. My sister, Rose, would have been the one to restore sanity in the family in her father's place with her previously established exuberant lifestyle, but her inexplicable demise has obliterated any comfort and recovery that would have been. Nonetheless, her emotional reactions on the loss of her nephew is remarkable. Of course, recognition of Delphine in this epistle is an obligation that cannot be ignored. Her innocence and shocking experience must not be what she bargained for, but she composed herself with a lot of mental aptitude and integrity.

So many people to thank, but if you don't find your name, it is because I didn't remember to include it on time for publication. Thank you, Daniel; thank you, Mike; thank you, Bill; thank you, Abdul; thank you, George; thank you, Nelson; thank you, Emmanuel; thank you, David; thank you, JJ; thank you, Brown; thank you, Rich; thank you, Francis; thank you, Sebastian; thank you, James; thank you, everybody!

Prince Kafain Emmanuel Mbeng, Sr. is a business management consultant who resides in Alexandria, Virginia, and operates an executive black car services in the Washington metropolitan area. He is also the president and CEO of KEMCO International, with headquarters in Belo-Boyo County in the Southern Cameroons. Prince Kafain, as he likes to be called, studied management science (BS) and marketing (MBA) at Southeastern University in southwest Washington DC. He is married and had two sons, Emmanuel K. Mbeng Jr. and Taku Mbeng before June 29, 2018, when death visited his home and painfully stole Junior away from him and his family—leaving him so devastated that he decided to share his painful emotional experience with the whole wide world in the hope that many parents will be warned never to take the time that they have with their children for granted, for they too could wake up one day and find them gone. *Painful Death: The Loss of a Child Is a Parent's Worst Nightmare* gives you Prince's personal insights on how to deal with the pain of such loss!

Prince Kafain Emmanuel Mbeng, Sr. was born into the Mbeng/ Chiabi family on Christmas Eve 1956 at the Banso Baptist Hospital in the grass fields region of the British Southern Cameroons, now called Ambazonia. His parents then took him to Baptist Teachers Training College, Great Soppo in Buea in the forest region, where they worked as teachers. In 1959, his father, Johnson M. Mbeng, left for further studies in Edinburgh, Scotland, during which time, his mother, Mary Bih, would take their three kids back to Belo, their native land in Boyo County. Then in 1962, when his father finally returned from Britain and took over the supervision of Baptist schools in the grasslands from an American Baptist missionary, Dr.

Gilbert Schneider, he moved his family to the Cameroon Baptist Mission center in Bamenda, where Prince Kafain and all his sisters attended the C.B.M. primary school. After completing class seven in June of 1969, Kafain's dad took him down to Cameroon Protestant College, Bali, and handed him over to Rev. Gordon, who was the Baptist vice principal of the school then, as was stipulated in the co-ownership agreement between the Baptist and Basel missions in Cameroon. Prince Kafain Emmanuel Mbeng, Sr. graduated from CPC in June of 1974, and, in 1975, was one of the pioneer students of the newly-opened government high school in Wum (Lycee de Wum) in Menchum Division.

Becoming one of the first Kom men to gain admission to study first in Nigeria, and then Edinburgh in Scotland, Prince Kafain's dad had sought to project a personal identity rather than become popular as prince of Kom. Prince's grandmother was a princess of Kom from the Kom palace in Liakom. Throughout his life, his dad incessantly hid behind this princely title, but after his death, his first son, Kafain, has now rightfully chosen to inherit this title of "Prince of Kom." And because Prince Kafain's maternal grandmother also hailed from the ruling royal house of Kom, Prince thus doubles as a member of the royal family that rules the Kom clan—a distinguished personality of pride in Kom citizenship and culture.

In his own right, Prince Kafain grew up quite a privileged kid, with many more amenities than most children his age. Living at the mission compound and having to play around with all the missionary kids was viewed by most of his other friends as a kind of nobility—a perception that made him uneasy and shy from the misconceptions that he was a famous and privileged kid. Prince hated such notoriety, and occasionally, some rough kids around would even chase and beat him around the school compound. But all the terror on him would be neutralized when Joel, his new best friend, would arrive from the Obudu Ranch in Cross River State across the northwestern border of West Cameroon. Joel, nicknamed Roy, had come from the Biafra war zone, and must have been emboldened by the war to be fearless. He defended and redeemed Prince from all these rascals. He brought a different kind of fame to Prince, who was now called "the kid with the strong friend." Roy possessed some macho moves that were attractive and protective and acceptable in their community of friends, and he immediately replaced every other kid-pal in Prince's world. The two of them bonded in character and style and have held on to this unique bond and brotherhood to this day.

In the sixties, and as a show of proficiency and respect for their supervisor of schools, teachers tossed Prince around in very many different ceremonial events. He was school band conductor at matches past, led the Boys Brigade at parades, cub scout flag-bearer at excursions, participant at all junior athletic events, forced onto traditional dance groups, and many others; and all these roles were just because teachers wanted to please his old man, who'd be seated in the front row at the ceremonial grandstands. At home, Prince was lucky enough to avoid regular house chores, like washing dishes and doing laundry, except when it was to dispel the myth of preferential treatment by his mother. He still had to make up his bed—a custom he hasn't broken to this day. The sentimental child that he was, and the kid in him, had some serious emotional issues though—issues that preoccupied his mind and played a vital role in the progresses that he made or failed to make every now and then. Only the people who actually knew him well—like his uncle, Dr. EML Chiabi, and his best friend, His Excellency Dr. Roy Joel N. Dimla—would be able to attest to his tale of emotional setbacks and the effects that these setbacks had on all of them. Everyone else saw Prince Kafain as this spoilt starlet, who was just waiting to excel. But he never let the fame of his times get to his head, and his outer frame never showed the inner feelings that got him by, within his circle of friends!

Struggling to find himself throughout life must be similar to what Prince believes his son was also dealing with, even if he, Junior, didn't tell him so. "The apple doesn't fall far from the tree," as some say, and the world in Prince's time was not as polarized as it is today. His boy was quite condescending, but not as much as he would have wanted him to be; nonetheless, he always had his back. As opinion-ated as Prince believed he was, his son emulated him. As reflective on family issues as he knew he was, Junior too was equally reflective; and only now has Prince come to the conclusion that child psychology and pedagogy is a much stronger virtue these days than what they experienced in their times. Pedagogy needs to receive the necessary attention it deserves if we want to avoid the kind of unforeseen circumstances that certainly caught Prince with his pants down.

Prince Kafain had returned from Nigeria, after missing matriculation into ABU, Zaria, where his best friend, Joel Dimla, was already studying. He eventually picked up a teaching job in BBSS, Soppo—the same school that his dad had taught at when he was a toddler. His "big brother," Bro. Richard, was the principal there at the time, and the school was now a secondary school. Due to some serious health issues with Bro. Rich, he and Prince got transferred to the Baptist Comprehensive College in Njinikejem-Kom. But an ambition for bigger things in Prince's life suddenly developed and exploded, superseding any desire to stay in a village community setting—even if it was meant to continue to give care to his brother, whom he loved passionately. That would become the reason why Prince would relocate to Douala, the economic capital of URC. After a very difficult stay there (details reserved), he subsequently landed on a big sales directorship at the Douala seaport, where he would raise enough funds to travel abroad in order to fulfill his own American dream. His time in Douala was quite interesting—needless to try to recount the enjoyment. And there were lots of exciting ventures and action to keep him there much longer, but not exciting enough to hold him back from joining his wanna-be with cousin, Victor, who had already abandoned his Cameroon bank job to pursue further studies in the States. The prospects of rising to the top in Cameroon were tellingly slim for Southern Cameroonians, and the roots of marginalization were just beginning to deepen deeper and deeper, resulting in the quagmire that is prevalently ripping the country apart today. Many years down the road in their Virginia residential rotations, Ka and Foin would propound a theory on stressful situations—probably from their financial duress—that "stress and pressure could slowly kill you, but stress and depression would slowly kill you faster." Prince Vic was quite fond of Prince Ka's jokes on an assortment of subjects and enjoyed his frequent expressions on such practical analytic truisms of life.

In the winter of 1983, Prince Kafain had thus taken off from the Douala International Airport, with a brief stopover at London-Heathrow International airport, finally landing at the Reagan National Airport in Washington, DC. He then joined Victor, who was still settling in to the beat of his new American life. Billy Jam, Ako Ayuk, and Eno Martin had helped to get him the I-20 from Southeastern University in DC, which Suki Martin brought to him in Douala a week before he departed. He would study management science (BS) and marketing (MBA) at SEU. But his anticipated return to the Cameroons, just as Cousin Vic's, and numerous others, would be impeded by the continuous marginalization, deprivation, discrimination, corrupt governance, and resource misallocation by LRC—marginalization that has consequently led to a struggle to restore the independence and self-determination of a people—the people of Southern Cameroons/Ambazonia. This status of independence was granted these English -speaking people by the United Nations in Resolution #1608 of 1961. This discrepancy has caused Prince and many anglophone Cameroonians to procrastinate their return home, if that would ever be possible. Most of them have established their families in the diaspora, with little or no desires to move back to their native homelands; and it may be important to note here that this influx and conduciveness has been on the rise, despite all the migration and immigration difficulties facing the world today. What a time to be caught between two presidencies, one making a mockery of perfectly established democratic institutions of government, while the other combining corruption and kleptomania with enlightened despotism or autocracy.

Prince Kafain went home to marry Junior's mother on December 19, 1992, the same day that his would-be best man had chosen for his own wedding in Lagos. Roy and Prince were out of communication for a while, due to communication difficulties of the times; but just like their baptism on the same day, they would pick the same day for their weddings. Interesting, right? And so Junior would be born ten months afterwards. That trip home in November of 1992 would also be Prince's first experience with the deteriorating state of affairs in the Cameroons since his departure to the States in 1983.

The political climate had become deplorable, and even his wedding ceremonies at the Ayaba Hotel were held under very high security, due to a declared state of emergency in Bamenda—the Northern Region's capital. Anglophones have always struggled to be relevant in their country, and at that time, it was about political parties and presidential elections. Of course, it has always been a one-man show there, and everyone else must either succumb or die. Prince's father had briefed him on the dangers of politics when he himself ran away from it in the early sixties, even though he tried to get back in at his old age; and now it was Prince fighting to pull him out of it. "It is a game, and one must play it smart or be bitterly crushed," the old man would say. Whether or not these trends are adorable is not the main concern here, but whether their people are free to exercise their rights to self-determination or self-governance is what is of paramount importance. Their children have become conditionally obligated to accept citizenship status as dictated to them by their uncertain but preferred choices, and at adult ages, they automatically integrate into socio-cultures that give them comfort and pleasure. Prince Kafain's boys actually wanted to break this cycle by eventually moving to the Southern Cameroons with him but were very worried about being able to cope there, after all the information they were receiving from their peers about all facets of the corrupt practices of life there.

Without the desire to be litigious or slanderous, Prince Kafain has tried to guide his boys in the right direction, but while we propose, God disposes. He has totally been aware of all the facetious consequences of behavioral science, and his JUNIOR was quite understanding of his plight, and often would use all his gravitas to circumvent his frustrations about life in general. They spoke the same language—the language of love of family—and Prince occasionally joked about how no one needed to be a rocket scientist to figure out that the universal language of family love matches only by the lingua franca of sex. So…the decision to indulge in this emotional presentation would live to be hailed by generations to come; for the uniqueness of the experience of the loss of child is challengingly abiding, but subjective to the individualistic discretions of time.

Prince Kafain has expressed himself in two other works: a fiction story, *EVEN LOVE CAN HURT YOU*, and a real-life experience, *CANCER DIAGNOSIS IS NOT A DEATH SENTENCE*. He possesses the love for writing and has an exciting way of retaining his readers' appetite when they read his books. He believes that a personal story like this current one would carry the same characteristics of inquisitiveness in the general public. He has thus provided readers with a desire to want to know more on how to deal with similar situations in their lives, which of course is why a recommendation is made for everyone to read every word of this brilliant expression of loss of child.

All said and done, an expression like this one underscores the importance of the relationship between parents and their children, and any sanctimonious misconceptions could allow cause to litigate a remorseful outcome. The actions of the parents are thus directly consequential on the behavior of their kids, and extreme precaution needs serious consideration every time there seems to be a breakage in this bond. Of course, this hypothesis may seem too late for Prince and JR, but courageously vital for all readers of this personal expression—or a wake-up call, so to speak!

Lightning Source UK Ltd.
Milton Keynes UK
UKHW021013111120
373191UK00007B/73